THE
MAXIMS
OF
MANHOOD

THE
MAXIMS
OF
MANHOOD

100 RULES
EVERY REAL MAN
MUST LIVE BY

JEFF WILSER

Avon, Massachusetts

Published by
Adams Media, a division of F+W Media, Inc.
57 Littlefield Street, Avon, MA 02322. U.S.A.
www.adamsmedia.com

ISBN 10: 1-60550-661-3
ISBN 13: 978-1-60550-661-6

Printed in the United States of America.

J I H G F E D C B A

Library of Congress Cataloging-in-Publication Data
is available from the publisher.

This publication is designed to provide accurate and authoritative information
with regard to the subject matter covered. It is sold with the understanding that
the publisher is not engaged in rendering legal, accounting, or other professional
advice. If legal advice or other expert assistance is required, the services of a competent professional person should be sought.
—From a *Declaration of Principles* jointly adopted by a Committee of the
American Bar Association and a Committee of Publishers and Associations

Many of the designations used by manufacturers and sellers to distinguish their
product are claimed as trademarks. Where those designations appear in this book
and Adams Media was aware of a trademark claim, the designations have been
printed with initial capital letters.

Interior illustrations © Neubau Welt (*www.NeubauWelt.com*).

This book is available at quantity discounts for bulk purchases.
For information, please call 1-800-289-0963.

To my father, stepfather, and grandfathers—all real men.

And to my mother, stepmother, and grandmothers—
who all had the misfortune of living with real men.

CONTENTS

ACKNOWLEDGMENTS

THESE WILL BORE you to suicide, so if you've never met me, skip it. You don't know these people, so why should you care? For real. Move on.

Thanks to Brendan for going to bat; Keith for the relentless encouragement and the 10,000 reads; Hakeem Olajuwon for '94 and '95; Wes for the Obi-Wan-esque theories on dating; Amy and Spencer for Garden Grill; Jamie for the Mile High support; Dan for the countless IM sessions; Sarah for the eagle editing eye; Kabir for bailing me out of jail; Terry and Braxton for a good hike; Jon Favreau for opening my eyes; Adam for the fantasy football smack-downs; Eric for the early days as a role model; Joe for being an ol' such-and-such; Saryn for the inspiration; Todd for doing well for himself; Gut for the SEG; Chuck for calling me Hixon; Tania for the legal counsel; Lisa/Shawn/Maya/Andre for the weekly focus; Cody for the parenting tips; James for being a dickhead; Evan for the good judgment; the whole crew at Track for a thrilling (if bizarre) ride; Erin for the patience; Stephane for the pep talks; Amanda for the call; A for believing; Sean for giving me a glimpse into the good life; Colleen and Lis for the great design; all my sisters for understanding; to Warren Moon for what might have been; and, finally, to Shannon M—whom I haven't seen in twenty years—for rejecting me in third grade and making me who I am.

INTRODUCTION

HERE'S THE THING about "real men" jokes: they're dumb. You know it. I know it. And any "real man" knows it. Let's be honest, okay? Why would a real man buy a book about being a real man? That's like God creating a Wikipedia page that tells Him how to invent the universe; it just doesn't pass the smell test.

Another thing about "real man" nuggets of wisdom: they're stale. Cliché. And they spawn from (often outdated) gender stereotypes. I mean, we get it, right? Old news. *Real men don't eat sushi.* Or *real men don't wear pink.* Or *real men can't recognize a salad fork, but they can operate a forklift.*

Western civilization, to some extent, has puzzled over the "real man" question for the last two, maybe three thousand years. From Aristotle to Hemingway to Burt Reynolds, it's some awfully well-worn territory.

So. Why this book?

Two reasons. The first of which is simple—analysis. Typically, a "man rule," or "man law," or "man code," or whatever, starts with the rule and ends with the rule. *A grown man may not use facial cream.* Fair enough. It has the whiff of authority; it makes you nod.

But . . . why? Isn't there some wiggle room, or at least some grounds for debate? Doesn't a real man want to attract real women, and if he has the facial complexion of Admiral Ackbar and discovers a miracle skin cream, wouldn't that be a good idea? Or is he just acting like a pansy, and a vain one at that? Where do you draw the line? (See MAXIM #41.)

The maxims tackle this gray area. They put the rules in perspective, show them in action, and yes, even consider the possible exceptions. Instead of being little sound bites that you tell your girlfriend, they articulate the reasoning, chew through the logic. They untangle the web of contradictions; they plunge deep into the nuance; they explore the tropes of masculinity. (Um . . . sometimes. When that shit fails, they make a bunch of *Seinfeld* and *Star Wars* jokes.)

The second reason for this book: evolution. Much of the conventional wisdom on "real man" topics, to put it delicately, is a crock of shit. We've evolved. The game has changed. Why can't men eat sushi? Girls like a man in pink (see MAXIM #45). And in this day and age, do we really need to know how to operate a forklift? I mean, *really*, a forklift? Isn't that why we go to college?

At the heart of the *Maxims of Manhood* is this core tenet: real men are not real idiots.

The modern man can read (MAXIM #62). He can even think (MAXIM #91). He can even, from time to time, show a flicker of compassion (MAXIM #29). And it's time that we acknowledge it. Instead of thumping our chests all cavemen style—"FIRE GOOOOD! EAT-RAW-FISH BAAADD!!"—it's time we create some new rules. More elevated rules. A code of behavior that has the brains to match its balls.

But let's not get carried away. Even though we're enlightened, real men are not real girly. So you'll recognize some of these maxims—the oldies but goodies—they're the golden truths that have been passed down from generation to generation. No matter how progressive our society becomes, you may never order a cocktail that's served with an umbrella (MAXIM #37). You know how to grill a steak (MAXIM #34). And your dog must be larger than a toaster (MAXIM #94).

The 100 maxims are broken into ten chapters, with ten rules per chapter: General Behavior, Sports, Women, Health and Food, Style, Work, Entertainment, Buddies, Women Revisited (a complicated subject), and some final edicts that defy classification. Most apply to all men. Some apply just to fathers, and some just to the single guys. Of course, single guys could one day become fathers—and vice versa.

You can read them in any order. A few are serious. A few are counterintuitive (MAXIM #91 on Supreme Court justices). And others serve the dual purpose of being both a "rule" and a sneaky, how-to piece of advice (like MAXIMS #26 and #81 on flirting).

Why am I qualified? I've met many men. I am one. And I've seen many men on TV, in movies, and even the occasional documentary. I've read about men—both fictional and real—in books, in essays, and sometimes (but less frequently) in plays. And I've written about them.

If that doesn't qualify me as the top expert on the planet, frankly, I don't know what would.

This book might not be for you.

It's only intended for people who fall into one of these seven buckets:

    (1.) You are a man.

    (2.) You will become a man.

    (3.) You were once a man.

    (4.) You are related to a man.

    (5.) You are dating or have married a man.

    (6.) You think that in the future, perhaps, you will date or marry a man.

    (7.) You know, or think that at some point you will know—whether casually or formally—a man.

If that's not you, stop reading.

If it is? On to the maxims . . .

PART I.
GENERAL BEHAVIOR

MAXIM #1

TIP WELL.

PROPER TIPPING SHOWS that you're worldly, you're not a tight-ass, and that, at rare moments, you even give a damn about people besides yourself. It's more than good manners—it's good ethics and it's good karma. You must know how to tip the following professions:

Barber: Simple common sense. You see the same guy at least once a month, so unlike at a restaurant, say, a frugal tip is neither anonymous nor forgotten. Ancient bit of wisdom: be generous to a man when he has a blade to your throat.

Hooker: For some reason the publisher denied my request for "research money" to explore this profession, but here's my hunch: if you tip a waitress 15 percent for serving you a plate of spaghetti, then you should probably tip a woman at least that much for letting you stuff her vagina with your penis.

Babysitter: She was just responsible for the life, safety, and health of the most important person in your world. If scorned, she's in a position to kidnap your baby. Probably not the best place to scrimp.

Church: On Sunday mornings, don't forget the donation buckets. God's done some good work for you. Tip Him at least 15 percent, or 20 percent if you've been particularly blessed.

Hot-dog dude at baseball game: Avoid public humiliation. A tip is not strictly required, but let's say the hot dog costs $4.25 (bargain!) and he passes it across a row of people. Now you *could* awkwardly shout over the crowd and ask for your seventy-five cents, but then you spend the next five innings being thought of as "That Guy."

Bartender: If the place is crowded, the key is to tip heavy *early* in the night, make eye contact, and they'll remember you later and give faster service. The better you tip, the better your odds of a buy-back.

Manicurist: I don't know this. And neither should you.

And don't forget the skycaps, valet guys, cabbies, dry cleaners, and bellhops. (Although you wouldn't use a bellhop, right?)

MAXIM IN ACTION

An unfortunate misconception that's surprisingly rampant: "I'll only tip the waiter for *good* service. They need to earn it." My friend Charlie only tips $2—regardless if the check was $8 or $80—thinking that the waitress is expending equal effort in both cases, so what's the difference? No need to cover ground better canvassed in *Reservoir Dogs*, but the basic fact is this: tips aren't simply icing on the cake for waitresses, they're part of a built-in assumption of income. They're taxed on it. They're counting on it for rent. Look at it this way: if we abolished the 15 percent rule of thumb (as Charlie would like), then the prices on the menu would be 15 percent higher. Do your part.

MAXIM EXCEPTIONS

The trend of some Starbucks, McDonald's, and Dairy Queens having the gall to place a *tip jar* on the counter is appalling, offensive, and a sign of the imminent collapse of Western civilization. They want a tip for serving a frickin' quarter-pounder with cheese? *Really?* This enrages you. This drives you batty. The fact you just spent the same amount of money on your quarter-pounder as you do for a beer—where you have no problem tipping—and the fact that this poor kid is working just as hard as the bartender . . . you find irrelevant.

MAXIM #2

YOU ONLY RECOGNIZE
PRIMARY COLORS.

THE MALE RETINA can only process three colors—red, blue, and yellow. Through heavy squinting, it is also possible, in rare and extraordinary circumstances, to recognize secondary colors like orange, green, and purple. Men can also understand black and white, as generations of watching football—natural selection—has developed an ability to spot the referee's uniforms.

Tragically, this physical handicap has been underreported by the mainstream media, triggering both miscommunication and awkwardness. Women will ask questions like, "What blouse should I wear: the periwinkle or the magenta?"

Periwinkle? Magenta? These words mean nothing. Magenta sounds like the villain from *X-Men*, the dude with the red and blue helmet (*maybe* you could call it purple). Periwinkle could be a Dickens character, or maybe a book by Dr. Seuss.

It's not that men simply *shouldn't* know the difference between "indigo" and "chartreuse," it's that we *don't*. Can't. It's not in our genetic code. And this impairment causes problems.

For instance, men are unable to enjoy picking out the color of new linoleum tiles. There will be no spirited debates over wallpaper. When you buy a car, you buy a red car, or a black car, or a blue car. Despite what it says in your owner's manual, your car sure as shit isn't "pewter." It's dark white.

MAXIM IN ACTION

Sometimes you'll see that guy who tries to rise above his physical limitations, which establishes a dangerous, uncomfortable precedent for the rest of our gender.

You've seen it. Your wife hoodwinked you into a trip to Linens and Things, and you overheard a guy say to his fiancée, "Oh, Sweetie . . . just look at this mauve pillow sham!" There are three problems with this exchange, not counting the "Oh, Sweetie." First, the guy shouldn't be the one pointing out pillow shams. Second, the guy shouldn't know what a "pillow sham" is. (A type of con or swindle, maybe, like a Ponzi scheme?) Third, of course, is "mauve." Maybe it's the original spelling of a desert in Utah, but it's not a color known to man.

MAXIM EXCEPTIONS

As a means of survival, men are required, from time to time, to construct the illusion of color comprehension. In the example, when the girl asks whether she should wear the periwinkle or magenta blouse, to cleverly dodge another argument, the guy might reply "periwinkle" with a reassuring nod, having no idea which one's which, and not even knowing if periwinkle refers to a color, fabric, or method of stitching.

Figure 1.2.
A red shirt.

And while scientists are still flummoxed by the exact nature of this paradox, it *is* possible for men to process nontraditional colors when they refer to sports teams. We can all agree that the Tide from Alabama is Crimson, not Red. Then again . . . if you see a Crimson Tide jersey out of context and can't see the logo or name, and someone asks you what color it is . . . you should know the only acceptable answer.

MAXIM #3

KNOW HOW TO GIVE
A COMPLIMENT.

SEEMS EASY. GIVING a compliment is simple. You just tell someone that they "did some good shit" or that they "look fucking good." What's so hard about that? The art of the compliment, however, requires a different approach for men and women, buddies and coworkers, family and strangers. While you're certainly not enrolled in the Ministry of Manners, you do know how to issue a compliment without kissing ass, embarrassing the recipient, or humiliating yourself.

You follow some basic Dos and Don'ts.

MAXIM IN ACTION

When complimenting a woman:

Do: Keep it simple. Avoid clichés. Hold eye contact. If you're in doubt? It won't score points for originality, but the old warhorse "You look great" has yet to fail.

Don't: Say that her breasts look terrific. Say she has beautiful eyes. (Barf.) Compliment her on the fine application of lipstick. Condescendingly say that she throws pretty well for a girl. Point at her dress and say, "Oooohhh, the new Betsey Johnson. Loves it!" (She wants you to appreciate how she looks in the dress. She doesn't want you to actually appreciate the dress itself. For women, fashion is a game of tricks and illusion. You just broke the spell.)

When complimenting a buddy:

Do: Understate it. If you're playing golf and he whacks a hole in one, your response should be something like, "That shot didn't suck." Compliment his new car, TV, gaming system, or power tool . . . even if yours is bigger and shinier and better.

Don't: Compliment his appearance (as per MAXIM #72). Say that his daughter is hot or call her a DILF. Tell your roommate that you heard the walls shaking all night, and it sounds like he's a real tiger in the sack.

When complimenting a coworker:

Do: Ensure the right person gets the right credit. Don't just lavish praise on the boss; speak up when the junior person worked until midnight. Acknowledge the behind-the-scenes stuff that gets overlooked.

Don't: Ever ask if someone "didn't get the memo" or refer to those "TPS Reports." No, these aren't compliments but they're very, very stale jokes. Telling them should be grounds for immediate dismissal. And you should never, ever compliment a woman's appearance in the workplace. You must act as if women look like pencil sharpeners: they're not pretty, not ugly; they're just competent, sexless machines that get the job done, same as a man.

When complimenting in the bedroom:

Do: Make her feel sexy. Compliment her body. Say that what she's doing feels good.

Don't: Overdo it. An unrelenting stream of flattery isn't sexy, it's corny. Just shut up and fuck already, okay? Another don't: if it's early in the relationship, you should never say "I love your body" or "I love the way you feel" or whatever. This is how it might sound to her: "I love . . . [long, dreadful pause] . . . your body." She might think you're about to drop the L-Bomb, in which case she'll either freak out or be disappointed. It's the same reason you should never give her jewelry that comes in a ring-sized box. A final don't: after oral sex, don't say, "I can tell you've done that a lot. You're a real pro."

MAXIM EXCEPTIONS

Less is more. You don't need to be frugal, per se, but if *every time* you see your girlfriend you say she looks beautiful, you assume the risk of sounding like a cheese ball. Compliments should never gush from your mouth like perfumed diarrhea.

MAXIM #4

NEVER SAY "BLOSSOM."

NOT ALL WORDS are created equal. They have connotations. Baggage. Words say more about you than your clothes, sunglasses, profession, or college diploma. Blindingly obvious? Maybe. But consider. Every year, millions of men shell out millions of dollars on John Varvatos suits, Tumi luggage, fashion magazines, and the like—all to improve their appearance. Fair enough. Yet how many of these same image-conscious men think about their vocabulary?

Which gets us back to the word "blossom." In a single day you could run a marathon, slay a wild boar, and uproot a tree with your bare hands. If, at the end of that day, you say to your wife, "Sugarplums, our little boy is really starting to blossom," you have just kneecapped an entire day of virility.

What if you're talking about the growth of flowers, which is an accurate, legitimate use of the word "blossom"? Strike two. Men don't talk about flowers. We're not aware if flowers blossom or wilt; we're only barely, grudgingly, aware of their existence.

But what if you're talking about actual "cherry blossoms"? Strike three. No man could point out a cherry blossom. Unless he's under physical duress, no man would even cop to knowing what a cherry blossom looks like. Is it a tropical plant? A dessert? A feminine hygiene product? We just don't know. It's like the etymology of San Diego—no one really knows.

Blossom is just an example. It headlines an entire echelon of words that should be avoided at all costs. Others include "okeydokey" (unless you're under 10 years old and have no friends), "delightful," "peachy," "lovely," "pizzazz," "hooray," and "treat." And don't forget "handsome." You have absolutely no reason to ever use the word "handsome."

Some questionable choices—use these at your own discretion— include "wonderful," "hooray," and "coolio." "Super" may be used as a prefix (as in "superstructure"), but not as an adjective ("Boy, that sure sounds *super*.")

MAXIM IN ACTION

The most flagrant violators of the "blossom" rule, weirdly, are football sportscasters. Otherwise manly men like Joe Buck will watch a cornerback blitz, let out an appreciative whistle, and marvel, "Boy, Jim, that number twenty-three has really blossomed into an All-Pro starting cornerback."

Um, guys? Remember your audience. Cornerbacks don't blossom. Men don't blossom. Little girls blossom into womanhood, a larva blossoms into a butterfly, and there's damn little reason for men to ever comment on larvae or butterflies.

MAXIM EXCEPTIONS

Sarcasm. When pulled off with just the right amount of scorn, you can get away with rolling your eyes and saying, "Yeah. That sounds like a real treat." Or you could say with a withering look, "Right. That'd be fucking *delightful.*"

This is especially permissible if you're rebuffing an idea that violates another maxim; like if your wife says, "Hey, honey, you've been watching the NFL draft for the last thirteen hours . . . why don't we put on *Pretty Woman?*" Yeah. That sounds like a real treat.

KEEP AN EMPTY URINAL BETWEEN YOU AND THE NEXT GUY.

IT'S SIMPLE PHYSICS. Leaving an empty urinal between you and the next guy, at its core, is a logical extension of Gay Lussac's Law—the 1809 physics theory—which posits that gases will expand when heated.

People seek space. You see it everywhere. In a crowded elevator, for instance, as some people exit, the remaining ones spread out, suddenly aware that they've been standing butt-to-crotch. At an empty beach, you wouldn't plop your blanket next to the only other dude. Sitting next to a stranger in a crowded movie theater? Normal. In an empty one . . . creepy.

This law applies to men, women, and—as Gay Lussac realized—atoms and molecules, too. It's universal.

So. Back to the toilet humor. Let's say you're in the men's room. You have a wall full of urinals to choose from. Most are empty. If you urinate next to the only one being used, you're making a *statement*. You're running against the grain of physics, violating the universe's very DNA. The poor guy with exposed sausage has every right to wonder: why?

Do you want to start a conversation? Idle chitchat is discouraged with penis in hand. Do you want to compare goods, size up the competition? You can do that online. Do you want to play a little "crossing the streams"? Just like in *Ghostbusters*, that results in "life as you know it stopping and every molecule in your body exploding at the speed of light."

MAXIM IN ACTION

Football games can cause trouble. Gay Lussac's 1809 experiment failed to consider the effects of alcohol and adrenaline, which temporarily offset our desire for space. As men stampede the bathrooms at Lambeau Field, say, their mutual outrage over a botched field goal might cause them—temporarily—to abandon decorum, urinate side by side, strike up conversations, and even break the ultimate taboo: make eye contact. This is the reason that sporting events stop selling alcohol in the fourth quarter.

MAXIM EXCEPTIONS

There is one scenario—and only one—that forces you to make a tough judgment call. Imagine that a bathroom has three urinals. Two are unoccupied. There's a dude using the one on the right. You'd use the one on the left, typically, to preserve your buffer. *But.* Now imagine this . . . the left-most urinal is a squatty little-boy urinal. Uh oh.

You have a dilemma. Both options are undesirable. If you go in the middle, you're encroaching the buffer zone. If you go on the left, you're a grown man who has chosen to pee-pee instead of piss.

What should you do? This, my friend, only you can answer. There are two schools of thought. An ideological schism, really. One camp contends that the buffer zone is inviolable, that you are to simply lower your trajectory and pretend you're only four feet tall. The other philosophy? That if you use the middle stall, the dude on the right will *know* it's because you're avoiding the toddler urinal, thereby absolving you of responsibility. He'll get it.

At what stage does life begin—conception, embryo, or birth? Does God exist? Middle stall or toddler stall? The three Big Questions. Choose wisely.

MAXIM #6

PACK TWO PAIRS OF SHOES
OR FEWER.

CAREFUL. THIS IS trickier than it looks. At first glance it seems simple: women pack too many shoes, men underpack, end of story, I get it, ha ha. What complicates matters, however, is that a conflicting theory states that like a good Eagle Scout, you should be prepared for anything, anywhere, always.

This creates a paradox. If it's manly to always be prepared, and it's *also* manly to carry around a heavy suitcase without wheels (for more on luggage and briefcases, see MAXIM #98) why wouldn't it be the peak of virility, therefore, to pack your entire closet—ski boots et al.—proving you can lug around 170 pounds without breaking a sweat or crushing your vertebrae?

Because overpacking violates a more fundamental principle: your healthy dose of not giving a shit. Like Tyler Durden from *Fight Club*, you have the "ability to let that which does not matter . . . truly slide." Overlooking the inconvenient fact that Tyler Durden either died or didn't actually, you know, *exist*, he articulates a key premise of our gender—superficial things are simply irrelevant, and stressing about shoes only obscures what's truly important.

Figure 1.6. *A complete wardrobe.*

By only packing two pairs of shoes you make a full-throated statement that you will not be fussy, you will not succumb to vanity, you will focus on your friends and your family and the fruits of your vacation. You have priorities. You will not get distracted with whether your tie matches your sneakers.

MAXIM IN ACTION

My buddy Todd visited me in New York one weekend. When we met at Grand Central, he wheeled a suitcase that looked like a foot-locker; it weighed eighty pounds and probably triggered some airport oversize fee. He said it was all essential.

At my place I watched him unpack, and he brought out jogging shoes (he doesn't jog), hiking boots (or hike), brown leather boat shoes (or boat), a windbreaker (this he does), a winter coat (in August), three ties (just in case), and—this is what got me—a pillow. A pillow! Why is a grown man traveling with a pillow? He said that he has trouble sleeping and that when he travels, he's more comfortable with his own feathery down. Todd has more trouble than sleeping. Learn from his failings.

MAXIM EXCEPTIONS

Destination weddings. Pretend you're a groomsman for a wedding in Puerto Vallarta. The weekend's activities include hiking, white-water rafting, golf, touring, dancing, and God knows what else. If you slavishly follow this rule, you're stuck wearing a tuxedo and beach sandals. Which, while amusing, will incur the bride's wrath and slap you with a lifetime friend probation. So when you have seven differ-ent photo-album events—with each of the seven events requiring a radically different outfit—then, and only then, may you pack more than two pairs. You get three.

MAXIM #7

OUTPERFORM THE GPS.

COMPUTERS HAVE THEIR uses. They can fetch stock quotes, calculate fantasy baseball stats, download porn, and maybe even a few other things. All things considered, men are okay with computers.

Until they overstep their bounds. When a GPS gives you directions that contradict your unfailing inner compass, you are right, the computer is wrong. Always. No collection of bits and bites, 1s and 0s, can possibly rival your lifetime experience of shortcuts, neighborhood savvy, and unerring nose for directions.

You are never lost. You are simply considering your options, weighing the pros and cons of turning left or right. Sometimes, even, it will appear to the uninformed passenger (wife or girlfriend, say), that you are "going in a circle," when really you are traversing more ground, gathering more data, shrewdly acquiring the lay of the land.

Trust your gut. The moment you start believing a computer over your highly evolved sense of direction—the moment you believe a blinking purple light over your foggy memory of where Baker Street might lead—is the moment you sacrifice your self-sufficiency, your very ability to survive.

Relying on the GPS breeds complacency, laziness. You actually *want* violent disagreements with the computer. It keeps you sharp. It reminds you—and your skeptical passengers—that when push comes to shove, you can get from A to B using your own wits. Even if it takes an extra hour.

It's a slippery slope. If you kneel to the GPS, soon you'll be riding around on those motorized scooters like Gob on *Arrested Development*, trusting a machine over your own two legs. You'll stop lifting weights and start using electronic muscle stimulators. You'll trust the low fuel indicator over your own hunch of how much gas you have left in the tank. You'll start reading instruction manuals. When your girlfriend tells you this is inconsistent with the maxim about you loving technology, you shake your head in disappointment. Again, she doesn't get it.

MAXIM IN ACTION

Like any corruption, it starts innocently enough. The guy will say, "Huh. I thought the side streets would be faster, so I can avoid traffic . . . but if the GPS says I should stay on the freeway, I guess I'll stay on the freeway."

The next trip, this guy's forgotten his local knowledge of side streets, his command of the city's traffic patterns. He stops watching the road. This isn't a man. This is a monkey pressing buttons. And soon he trusts the gadget like it's flashing text messages from God.

MAXIM EXCEPTIONS

If you're driving in someone else's car and using their GPS, decorum permits you to humor them. Follow the flawed instructions and pretend to marvel at the computer's slickness, even as you silently chuckle, knowing you're right and it's wrong.

Another exception. If you've never been to a particular geographic region, the GPS is a perfectly valid tool. That's its main purpose. Its *only* purpose. You can let the GPS be a tour guide, of sorts, mapping out this new swath of land.

However, once you've driven on a street—and once is all it takes—you are now more of an expert than the GPS. From that point forward, when you have the slightest inkling that you should go north when the computer says south, that spidey sense of yours is 100 percent accurate—even if doesn't appear that way. Have faith in your convictions. Remember: everyone said Galileo was wrong, too.

MAXIM #8

USE THE DIAPER BAG
ONLY FOR DIAPERS.

IT'S UNAVOIDABLE. WHEN you spawn a child, you'll be obligated to wipe her poop, clean her vomit, and scrape her mucus from the remote control. Which is fine. That goes with the territory. But something else awaits you, something far more troubling: the diaper bag.

You're allowed to wear a diaper bag. Don't let anyone knock it. Sure, maybe it looks a little sissy, but it's the ultimate symbol of your virility—triumphant proof of the power of your loins. You did it. You impregnated a woman. On purpose, even! So you wear that diaper bag, and you wear it with honor.

Yet you must avoid the following temptation. That diaper bag will have several pouches. One of the pockets is just the *perfect* size for your cell phone. It could also fit your wallet. Maybe, even, it could hold your car keys. A pack of gum. Your iPod.

Don't do it. This is a line you must not cross. The second you put your cell phone in the pocket, it stops becoming a diaper bag and starts becoming a purse. You're no longer the proud father—you're a dude carrying a purse. The diaper bag may contain one thing and one thing only: diapers.

Figure 1.8.
A slippery slope.

Similarly, you'll be intrigued by ads you see for "messenger diaper bags." Some of them have funky logos and graffiti designs—the kind of thing you'd get if you were seventeen and just discovering the Ramones. They come in camouflage, flames, and even skull and crossbones.

You know what? You're not seventeen (hopefully). You've already discovered the Ramones. You have a baby. You're a grownup. Own it. Live it. Don't seek apparel that makes you more of a kid and less of a man. (For more on dressing your age, see MAXIM #48).

17

MAXIM IN ACTION

One brand advertises on its website: "Little Dudes and Divas specializes in designer diaper bags and diaper bag accessories. We bring you the latest in designer diaper bags. Our brands include Mia Bossi, Holly Aiken, Fleurville, Room Seven . . ." No. Unless you pattern your manhood after Miley Cyrus, you refuse to purchase daddy gear from a boutique called "Little Dudes and Divas."

MAXIM EXCEPTIONS

If your diaper bag's a backpack? You're off the hook. You can stuff it with power bars, cell phones, magazines, keys, or porn. A rational, dispassionate onlooker might wonder why it's acceptable to put keys in a backpack but not in a diaper bag. Because of the magical second strap. The second strap takes any bag and transforms it from a purse to backpack. Another exception: if the health of your child is contingent on you storing something in the diaper bag, it's generally permissible to value the baby's life over your ego. Usually, though, you can stuff any baby items in your pockets. Yes it's uncomfortable. But as my buddy Cody says, "Holding an uncomfortable amount of stuff in your pockets is your way of suffering. It's the male version of childbirth."

MAXIM #9

CELEBRATE BIRTHDAYS LIKE YOU CELEBRATE TUESDAY.

YOU LOVED BIRTHDAYS. You loved the pageantry, the fun and games, the great whoosh of excitement. Ice-cream cakes. Gifts. Surprise parties. You loved all of it.

Then you turned twelve. Suddenly, you weren't as easily charmed by a grown man who can juggle, loaf around in floppy shoes, and twist balloons into implausibly skinny elephants. Clowns became creepy. Cakes became cheesy.

Since then, it hasn't been the same. From time to time, of course, you've observed birthdays, and you've gone through the motions. Sure, some have been epic. Like your twenty-first, when your friends encouraged you to pound twenty-one shots—one for each hour in the emergency room.

These days, however, you only celebrate birthdays when absolutely necessary. Even then, "celebrating birthdays" with your buddies, really, is just code for grabbing a few pitchers. You celebrate birthdays like you celebrate Tuesday.

Things you will *not* do for birthdays:

You won't buy your buddy a cake. This is a dramatic contrast from girls, who still adore the idea of blowing out candles, wearing goofy pointy hats, and singing "Happy Birthday" like we're on *Romper Room*.

You won't remember your friend's birthday. It'll come up in conversation three weeks after the fact, and you'll say something like, "Oh. Right. Happy Birthday, dude." He won't be insulted. You won't be embarrassed. Because male friendships don't stand on ceremony.

You won't forget your girlfriend's birthday. You can't. It's impossible, because she's reminded you thirty-seven times. First, you get the nine-month reminder—a casual "Oooooh, that antique typewriter would make a *peerrrrfect* birthday present!" Then you get the three-month alarm, a more urgent reminder about clearing your schedule. Soon it escalates to weekly, then daily conversations about the Big Day, serving as an annual dress rehearsal, of sorts, for your Wedding Planning (see MAXIM #25). You remember her birthday like a diabetic remembers to check his blood sugar: you have no other choice.

MAXIM IN ACTION

Girls don't just have birth*days*, they have birthmonths. They have the pre-birthday dinner, then the birthday night-clubbing, then the post-birthday brunch. And that's just for the in-town friends; they'll also have birthday cocktails a week earlier (and a week later) to squeeze in any visiting girlfriends or relatives. You? Celebrating a birthday for an entire month is fine, you think, as long as you're the actual Son of God.

MAXIM EXCEPTIONS

Some birthdays carry weight. Your twenty-first. Your thirtieth. Even your fortieth. For these exceptional milestones, you've accrued enough not-giving-a-shit points to splurge a little when it counts. Another exception: family. Even though you believe there's zero correlation between mailing a card and your love for your mother (cards are something that women mail BFFs they're not friends with anymore), totally flaking on your parents' birthday will cause, at best, a misunderstanding. I've whiffed all four of my parents' and stepparents' birthdays. It's never a good feeling. One year I remembered my mom's two days too late. I called her in cold panic, ashamed. She answered the phone laughing. "I just felt bad for *you*," she said. Wait, she felt bad for *me*? Why? "I knew that as soon as you remembered," Mom said, "you'd feel really mad and disappointed in yourself, so I felt bad for you." Even when your mom's as cool and understanding as mine, never forget her birthday.

MAXIM #10

NEVER TAKE SIDES AGAINST THE FAMILY.

From *The Godfather*:

"A man who doesn't spend time with his family
can never be a real man."
—Don Corleone

"Fredo, you're my older brother, and I love you.
But don't ever take sides with anyone against the family again. Ever."
—Michael Corleone

IF YOUR FAMILY is anything like the Corleones, when you take sides against the family you get a bullet to the head. The other ninety-nine maxims are breakable. This one is not. Your fidelity to your family trumps your job, your career, your every ambition in life.

Obviously your family is the best family in the world and the best family in history (except mine), and you are, by extension, the greatest father in the world. But you've learned a thing or two from other dads out there. Each one has a singular quality to incorporate into your parenting.

MAXIM IN ACTION

Father: Darth Vader
Quality: Efficiency

Say what you want about the whole turning-to-the-dark-side kerfuffle, but give him credit for this: he only saw his kid "with his own eyes" for a total of seven seconds, but that was enough for some quality father-son bonding. They healed. No matter what you do, no matter how many Jedi you slaughter, your kid will find the good in you.

Father: Jor-El
Quality: Wisdom
Damn. Now *this* is a dad who knows his shit. He doesn't just give his son a few scraps of advice, he gives him the *sum total of intergalactic knowledge*, which anticipates, apparently, every possible conflict his son could ever possibly encounter.

Father: Jim's Dad from *American Pie*
Quality: Wholesomeness
Admit it. This stuff's awkward. When you think about having the "sex talk" with your son, you're not sure if you should talk about the birds and the bees or how to locate the clitoris. Jim's Dad gets it.

Father: Kyle Reese from *The Terminator*
Quality: Solidarity
The dude was such good friends with John Conner, he volunteered to go back in time and screw his buddy's mother so he could be his buddy's dad. That's friendship.

Father: Jack Byrnes (De Niro in *Meet the Parents*)
Quality: Protectiveness
No tactic is too ruthless. The end always justifies the means. Jack Byrnes is a man who keeps his daughter off the pole (MAXIM #95).

MAXIM EXCEPTIONS

"The Family" vs. "Not The Family" is an easy call. "Family Group A" vs. "Family Group B" is messy. You want complicated? I have three "double-stepsiblings" in that my dad is married to their mom, my mom is married to their dad. (Think about that for a second.) Growing up together, despite all of our best intentions—and despite the fact that we all love each other and all that—the appearance of "taking sides" is inevitable. Fights are inevitable. Frosty tension is inevitable. And this is why every happy family has a happy stock of wine.

PART II.
SPORTS

MAXIM #11

NEVER SWITCH YOUR
FAVORITE TEAM.

YOU WILL HAVE many jobs. You will own multiple cars, pets, and suits. And barring some nightmare scenario where you marry your high school sweetheart, you'll go from girl to girl.

Like almost everything else in life, these are all fleeting. Replaceable. But you do have something timeless and true, a lifelong bedrock: your favorite sports team. You are permitted one team for each major sport, and this can never change. Ever.

Your girlfriend won't get it. She'll ask, "Wait, didn't you say you have 'commitment issues'?" She'll then argue, "If the whole point of sports is a fun diversion, why not just root for whomever you please, sip your beer, and enjoy the game?"

You know better. Sports aren't just some "fun diversion." Every year is a long, torturous season, where you slog through bad drafts and crushing playoff defeats. We lose more than we win. We sulk more than we cheer.

This pain, though, is like boot camp for our soul. It hardens us. It steels us for life's disappointments. To flinch from this pain—to upgrade teams when your beloved Falcons are in the gutter—is to betray your core principles. The man who changes teams cannot be trusted. This is the man who flip-flops his politics and cheats on his wife.

The maxim transcends geography. If you grew up in Boston as a lifelong Patriots fan, and then you have the misfortune of moving to Buffalo, it is unacceptable to adopt the Bills as your new team. It also transcends individual players. True, a Packers fan is allowed to root for Brett Favre when he plays for New York, but he is forbidden from claiming the Jets as his new favorite team.

A note on timing. You might wonder when in life, precisely, you need to make your choice. Follow this rule of thumb: you should settle on your favorite team by the day you stop trick-or-treating. When you've stopped dressing up like Yoda to beg your neighbors for fun-sized Kit-Kats, you've entered the grown-up world of sports fidelity.

MAXIM IN ACTION

We see it every year. When the Celtics acquired Kevin Garnett in exchange for Al Jefferson, Ryan Gomes, and a sack of magic beans, it was miraculous how many "die-hard" Celtics fans emerged from the woodwork. Or how when the Giants won the Super Bowl, millions claimed they had "never stopped believing" . . . except, say, between the years 1991 and 2008. Be a man and root for a losing team. It makes you a hard, jaded cynic.

MAXIM EXCEPTIONS

Remember the Houston Oilers? Los Angeles Rams? Minnesota North Stars? They all had loyal(ish) followings. For these teams, the greedy owners are deadbeat dads: they ditch town for a creamy young mistress, higher revenue, and a gleaming new stadium. As with any deadbeat dad, they leave behind a confused, fatherless, vulnerable child. When you are that trembling child, when your franchise abandons you, then—and only then—do you have permission to seek a new team. But don't get carried away. This isn't some lifelong get-out-of-loyalty free card. While the emotional scars take some time to heal (as a Warren Moon–loving Houston Oilers fan, I know they never fully heal), you should make your choice within eighteen months of your old team's final game.

MAXIM #12

AVOID KICKERS IN THE FIRST ROUND.

MANY YEARS AGO in a less civilized society, we discovered a small problem with football: in some games, we didn't really care who won. We got bored. When the games were uncompetitive, we'd even think, fleetingly, about spending Sundays with our family.

This was unacceptable. So we created Fantasy Football, ensuring that every game, no matter how inconsequential, would become life's top priority. Colts 67, Redskins 3? If you have Peyton Manning and you're down by four, you'll skip your girlfriend's birthday to watch *Monday Night Football.*

With great diversion comes great responsibility. Fantasy Football has its own code of honor and decorum. For starters, don't be *that guy* who reaches too early for a kicker. Do your homework. No, you don't need a geeky binder of spreadsheets (I'm looking at you, Adam), but you must know the basics: running backs early, tight ends late.

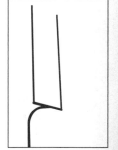

Figure 2.2.
Sunday church.

You are expected to stay competitive. Even if your team is a doormat with no mathematical shot of making the playoffs, you are forbidden from becoming an absentee owner, starting quarterbacks with torn ACLs.

You are expected to trash-talk. Routing your buddy is only half the battle—you must also insult his tactics, judgment, character, sister, demeaning job at Initech, and overall lot in life. You can't just "win"; you must make him feel small. You must break his spirit. Conversely, when the insults are lobbed in your direction, you are never allowed to take it personally.

MAXIM IN ACTION

Okay. I'll admit it. I'm a little biased in my zealotry. I started my league back in high school, way, waaaay before its popularization via ESPN. In Latin class, I hid the sports section under Caesar's *The Gallic Wars*, using a calculator to tally up the box scores. Back then people hadn't even *heard* of Fantasy Football, so I'd awkwardly explain to classmates, "No, you're not exactly 'fantasizing' about the players . . ."

Now? My high school buddies have all scattered from Houston to Los Angeles, New York, Spokane, and Terre Haute. Some are still bachelors, some have kids, some rich and some poor, some Republicans and some Democrats.

There's only one thread that keeps us in touch: Fantasy Football. It gives us an excuse to bullshit, to swap stories, to reminisce about a golden era, a time before diapers and 401(k)s. Girls have emotions; guys have third-string running backs. Let's not rock the boat.

MAXIM EXCEPTIONS

Technically there is no exception to the "no kicker in first round" maxim, but there is one overall caveat. In case of a conflict, you must always root for your real NFL team over your fantasy team. Let's take an example. If you're an Eagles fan and they're playing the Bengals— and you have Carson Palmer as your starting quarterback—you must root for Palmer to throw five interceptions, even though your fantasy team is kneecapped. Your real team comes first, even though it's emotional anguish, even though it's the guys' version of *Sophie's Choice*.

MAXIM #13

SHUN NETWORKING GUY.

WHEN YOU GO to watch a game, you must go to *watch the game*. You're not there to woo a client. You're not there to lather up your boss. You refuse to be Networking Guy. You shun him.

Additional in-game etiquette:

No cussing in front of the kids. I'm fucking serious. You can be as raunchy as you'd like in the sports bar, but when you're in earshot of little Timmy, trade the shits for shoots. Plus, it's fun. My favorite trick is to swap well-known profanity with unique, G-rated slurs. Like when the ref makes a bad call you scream, "Awww c'mon, ref, that's a bunch of HORSE . . . RADISH!!!" Or you can say the call wasn't bullshit, it's "baloney." Try it sometime. You're guaranteed a chuckle.

That being said, tolerate loudness. Embrace it. Don't be that guy shhhhhshhing the crowd. You're at a stadium. Deal with it. If you want to watch a game in complete silence, go see the Toronto Raptors.

A word on jerseys. If you're at a Cubs/Astros game, minus 5 points for wearing a Braves jersey. (Wrong team.) Minus 10 points for wearing a Bulls jersey. (Wrong sport.) Minus 35 points for wearing an Argonaut jersey (Wrong country.) Minus 100 points for wearing a custom, personalized jersey with your name on it. (Wrong path you've chosen in life.)

Do not do The Wave. It's now in the highest pantheon of group corniness, right up there with the Macarena and YMCA. If the rest of the stadium starts it? Stand your ground. Follow your principles. Be that lone, defiant protestor in Tiananmen Square, staring down the tank that is the wave.

Unless you're eight years old, no bringing your glove to a baseball game. Two words: Steve Bartman. If he had followed this maxim in 2003, his Cubs might have won the World Series.

MAXIM IN ACTION

You can't miss them. The two guys sitting right in front of you, blocking your view of the end zone. They're wearing suits and clacking on their BlackBerries. Every once in a while, when the crowd roars, they glance at the field in confusion. You overhear a snippet of their conversation and hear them mention the "second quarter"; you're pleasantly surprised—maybe they're actually paying attention. Then they say, "By the second quarter of next year, the tax credit from our depreciation . . ." and you realize they can't name the starting quarterback.

MAXIM EXCEPTIONS

The WNBA. If you somehow get suckered into watching the Liberty Sparks, do whatever you must to stay awake. Toss out the rules. You're off the hook. Reorganize your phonebook, reconnect with third cousins, call your old kindergarten buddies. Network. Bring along your laptop, even, and knock out that PowerPoint presentation. Finally sink your teeth into Tolstoy. Listen to a podcast. Learn to juggle. Clip your toenails. Anything goes: it's the WNBA.

MAXIM #14

KNOW WHO'S PITCHING.

LET'S SAY YOU'RE a Dodgers fan. It is unacceptable for you to walk into a buddy's apartment, see they're playing on TV, and casually ask the room, "Hey. Who's pitching tonight?" Or, even more appalling: "Hey guys. Who are we playing?" ("We," apparently, are playing a little game where we pretend that we're a sports fan and have a penis.)

No actual fan would be so blithe, so oblivious, about who's playing or who's pitching. It's like Sarah Palin never having heard of the Bush Doctrine. These are simply things you *know*. How could you not?

MAXIM IN ACTION

You know your team. Specifically you know the following:

Your team's schedule. No, you don't need to be the anal-retentive dork who memorizes the Raiders' entire sixteen-game schedule, but you must, at a minimum, know the next few games. You should know upcoming opponents, any scheduling quirks (night game vs. day game), and you should know when your team is on bye, because that's the one weekend between Labor Day and February that you can spend Sunday with your girlfriend.

Your team's roster. It's amazing how many "fans" will watch a football game and have utterly no clue who's anchoring the O-Line. You might not know the names of all your cousins, but you know all fifty-three players, and you know where they went to college.

Your team's strengths. This is more encouraged than required. While you don't have to be an Xs and Os wizard like Hubie Brown or Ron Jaworski, you should be able to talk a little strategy. You should know that when you match up against the Warriors, you have a height advantage and should dump the ball in the post.

Your team's weaknesses. There aren't any. These guys are going all the way.

Your team's coach. You're smarter than the coach. You know that he should have gone for it on fourth down, that he should start the rookie quarterback, and that he's deploying the prevent-defense alarmingly too early. Yes, you acknowledge that he watches fifty hours of game film a week. But that just makes him blind to the obvious.

Your team's history. It separates the bandwagoners from the faithful. Without hesitating, you can rattle off the years your team won a title, the years they should have, and 80 percent of the championship starting lineups.

MAXIM EXCEPTIONS

You get a pass if you haven't hit puberty. Alternatively, if your old team ditched you (see MAXIM #11), you have a fleeting excuse for ignorance. But get with the program, okay? Hit the books and learn your team. A third exception: if it's a borderline sport that only merits passing interest, then only cursory knowledge is necessary. These include wrestling, track, tennis, the Olympics, Ivy League college football, and any sport involving women. (See the front of the book for where to send hate mail.)

MAXIM #15

SLAP HIS ASS.

PHYSICAL AFFECTION WITH another man freaks you out.

The idea of holding a man's hand is unthinkable. You'd never help a man comb his hair. You wouldn't kiss him on the cheek. You wouldn't rub sunscreen on his back.

Obvious stuff, right? These taboos are so off-limits, so clearly beyond the pale, that they don't even warrant their own maxims. You get it. Even though the infractions seem minor—and even though, frankly, it's the same harmless stuff that girls do with girls—you don't want to go there because, you know . . . well, *you know.*

So you avoid physical contact with other men. (For the special case of male-hugging, see MAXIM #76). You keep them at arm's length. Good for you and good for him. Good for all of us.

Except . . .

When you're both hot and sweaty and playing the same sport, nothing is more emphatically, more clearly heterosexual than slapping another man's ass. When he hauls in a touchdown, you slap him on the ass. When he swishes a three-pointer, you pat him on the ass. When he smacks a home run, you treat his butt to a little palm lovin'. Even when he *misses* a free throw, you still say to yourself "You know what? Screw it! Let's slap him on the ass!"

And this doesn't strike you—or anyone—as at all homoerotic. Trying on another man's pair of jeans? That's gay. Tapping the man's butt? That's camaraderie.

One theory . . . Your athletic prowess is so virile, so stunningly heterosexual, that it gives a smoke-screen for everything and anything else. And who knows? Maybe the ass tap is just the beginning. Soon, perhaps, we'll see more advanced moves—when the pitcher throws a no-hitter, say,

Figure 2.5.
Crossing the line.

his teammates all line up and give him the newest gesture of manly appreciation: the "ball squeeze."

MAXIM IN ACTION

Just flip on a football game. Check out your neighborhood basketball courts. Or, better yet, watch the beach volleyball scene from *Top Gun*, which gets the Lifetime Achievement Award for "Gayest Scene in the Straightest Movie." In glorious slow-motion (and to the song "Playing with the Boys"!), Val Kilmer and Tom Cruise get half naked, glisten with sweat, high-low-five and butt-tap their way to hetero box-office triumph.

That was straight. But if Maverick asked Goose to spread some sunscreen on his back, for the legitimate reason of not getting a sunburn? Now that's a little . . . *you know*. Keep the hetero affection where it belongs—on another man's butt.

MAXIM EXCEPTIONS

Technically, this entire maxim is an exception to a more global one: minimize physical contact between men. When you're feeling sleepy on the bus, no resting your head on your buddy's shoulder. Avoid cuddling. Unless it's after a big win. Then you can strip off your jersey and join many men in a big pile on the floor . . . because a sports-related group man-orgy cuddle isn't a cuddle—it's a huddle.

STAY UNTIL THE END.

IF SPORTS WERE merely about jumping and sweating and catching balls, we'd be just as entertained watching dogs play fetch. But we demand more. Strategy, pushing the limits, heart, redemption, and every once in a long, long while . . . moments of magic.

We crave this magic. The stunning comebacks, like Tracy McGrady's thirteen points in thirty-three seconds. Eli Manning and the helmet catch. The Sox coming back from 0–3. The Bills roaring back from thirty-two points against Warren Moon and the Oilers. And so on.

This magic doesn't come free. The price is loyalty. To truly appreciate these golden moments, you must demonstrate your commitment. When you pay good money to cheer the home team, it is unacceptable to leave early to beat traffic. Your team deserves better. You deserve better.

The deserters who skulk out of the stadium with six minutes left—bowing their heads in shame, peeling off their jerseys—should be photographed by security, have their tickets confiscated, and get slapped with a lifetime ban from the ballpark.

Would you walk out of your daughter's piano recital the moment she flubs a key? Abandon your buddy if he passed out in the bar? Ditch your girlfriend if she suddenly became annoying? (Scratch that last one.)

MAXIM IN ACTION

The traffic-beater species is not indigenous to any one city. They're everywhere. They flee blowouts; they wince at the first drops of rain. Some traffic-beaters actually leave early during *close* games, perhaps because they forgot their Midol.

The problem is exacerbated in large cities like L.A. and New York, where the fourth quarter means giant swaths of empty seats. No city is immune.

Take Denver. In October 2007, the Chargers thumped the Broncos 41–3, and the Bronco "faithful" trickled out of the stadium early in the third quarter, leaving behind an empty stadium of just a few fans—mostly visiting Chargers fans. The players noticed. Specifically, wide receiver Brandon Marshall noticed.

"If you're going to be a Broncos fan, be a Broncos fan. Don't boo us when we're down. That's bandwagon," said Marshall. "When we start winning, then what? I love you all to death, but at the same time, that's not first class. . . . When we're losing, you all stay in those seats."

MAXIM EXCEPTIONS

When your team works for you—winning or losing—you root for them. It's simple. It's fair. Sometimes, though, the team doesn't hold up its end of the bargain. If the coach surrenders at an embarrassingly early point in the game—yanking the starters in the third quarter, say—they've done little to earn your continued interest.

Sometimes booing is in order. Sometimes genuine rage, disgust, calling for the coach's scalp, and yes, if the players have lost interest, quit, and started fondling their iPhones on the sidelines—sometimes leaving early is in order. When NBA cellar-dwellers openly tank games in April, you have a right to voice your disappointment. Make no mistake. This extraordinary circumstance is a protest, a last resort, going nuclear, a way of rebuking a child whom you otherwise love.

MAXIM #17

MAKE YOUR SON A LEFTY.

YOU TAKE THE long view. Sure, maybe when you're a little kid being left-handed makes it harder to learn writing, gets you laughed at, and causes you to wonder, "Am I *different?* Am I weird?" All of this awkwardness pays off, however, when your son is old enough to play sports, and especially when he goes pro. (Which your kid will. You just feel it.)

Lefties are treasured. Lefty pitchers, lefty batters, lefty tennis players—it's a lethal advantage. If a college is awarding one baseball scholarship and they're choosing between two equally talented pitchers—one right-handed, one left-handed—they'll choose the lefty. Each and every time. Babe Ruth, John McEnroe, Oscar de la Hoya, Randy Johnson, Rocky Balboa? All southpaws.

Figure 2.7.
Your son's future profession.

You want this advantage for your son. Therefore you channel your inner Mr. Miyagi and do whatever it takes to *make* him left-handed, starting at the earliest possible age. You're confident that nurture can trump nature.

So you'll force your kid to write with his left hand, even when he just scribbles and cries and says it doesn't feel good. Same with drinking milk, using the mouse, and brushing his teeth. When he goes to the bathroom, you teach him the left-hand-wiggle.

MAXIM IN ACTION

My dad was all about the long view. This doesn't apply to southpaws, per se, but it's the same overarching philosophy: your kid will suffer so that he (might) be happier later in life. When our family moved from New York to Texas, a weird quirk in the school calendar meant that I could either join kindergarten or first grade. My parents gave it lots of thought. They ran through all the scenarios. My dad decided on first grade. His logic? Since I would be a year younger than my classmates every grade for the next sixteen years, I would benefit—despite the social awkwardness—by graduating college a year earlier and, therefore, have one additional year of "earning power" (Dad's exact words) before I retire and die. Now that's the long view.

MAXIM EXCEPTIONS

If your son doesn't have a lick of interest or aptitude in sports, you might abandon the southpaw strategy. At that point, however, you'll be desperate for *any* flicker of curiosity, and you'll delude yourself into thinking he just hasn't found the "right" sport. When he can't dribble a basketball (even with your assistance) or catch a baseball (even when you toss it underhand from three feet away), you decide triumphantly that, "Ah ha! He must be into track and field," and you make the poor little bugger run laps until he collapses, cries, and almost passes out from heatstroke. Because you know what's good for him.

YOU'RE IMMUNE TO COLD.

THE COLD DOESN'T bother you. It never has. You were cold once—*once*—when skiing a black diamond. Double-diamond, actually. In a blizzard. And even then, come to think of it, you wouldn't have been all that cold, but you loaned your gloves and hat to your girlfriend, and then ice trickled down your chest. You were cold for approximately ten minutes, then you got moving and warmed up just fine.

It's not just a metaphor: we have thick skin. We're physically incapable of ever being colder than the girl. When we give the girl a jacket, it's actually doing *us* a favor, unburdening us of a superfluous layer of clothes.

And if we look cold? You're mistaken. We're not shivering. We're laughing. Our shoulders are shaking in mirth; we're just so amused that someone else could consider this weather—a pleasant twelve degrees—the slightest bit uncomfortable.

MAXIM IN ACTION

A one-time violator: me. I was white-water rafting at my buddy Jamie's bachelor party. There were seven other guys in the raft. Good times all around—warm sun, crystal clear water, bullshitting, the last gasps of freedom with a few good friends. You could almost hear the soundtrack of a beer commercial.

Then it started raining. And got cold. As we paddled and paddled, the water splashed in the raft and drenched our shirts. Morale plummeted; no one spoke. You could hear eight sets of chattering teeth.

Earlier in the day, our rafting guide (a big hairy dude named "Ewok") told us he had a bag full of rain slickers and fleece. As the rain fell I eyed the bag longingly, wondering when he'd bust out the jackets. He didn't. The sky darkened. It got colder.

I couldn't take it anymore. If the fleece was in that bag—right in front of us, right there!—um, why not use it? Common sense, right? I set down my paddle and turned to Ewok. "So . . . maybe I'm breaking rafting code, but can I have one of the jackets?"

You'd think I'd asked if I could sit on his lap and rub his belly. He was stunned. The other guys—equally freezing and miserable—burst out laughing and gave me shit. Finally Ewok blinked, muttered something to himself, and rummaged in the bag and pulled out a fleece. (Turns out he had only brought one.)

If you're still out there, Ewok, this rule's for you.

MAXIM EXCEPTIONS

If you're actually suffering from frostbite, you may ask for a sweatshirt. There's no reason to complain about your frostbite, though: make the best of it. If you have trench foot, no one will fault you for getting new shoes. Except Ewok.

MAXIM #19

NO GRANNY SHOTS.

FOR THE UNINITIATED: the granny shot is when you scoop the basketball with both hands, hold it between your squatting legs, then toss it in the air the way you might heave a microwave. It's undignified. It's unseemly. It looks like you've never even watched the game of basketball, much less played it.

It's unacceptable. This doesn't mean that you have to shoot a Steve Nash–like 90 percent from the charity stripe. But you need the basics. Shooting a basketball is Guy 101. Similarly, you must demonstrate proficiency—even if it's just rudimentary—for the following:

Tackle. The metaphor's sort of painfully obvious, but that doesn't make it any less true. Tackling shows that you can meet a problem squarely, unafraid to get hurt or get dirty. The guy who refuses to tackle is the guy who ducks a fight, dodges the draft, and skips his alimony.

Run a mile. You're allowed to huff and puff. And you don't have to run the 40 in 4.3 seconds. But at the very least, you must be able to jog a mile without looking like Chunk from *Goonies*.

Do a pull-up. If Linda Hamilton can do several pull-ups in *T2*, you should at the very least be able to do one. Palms out, straight waist, no bucking.

Throw a baseball. You'll never outgrow this. Long after those sunny days at Little League, you'll still be faced with company picnics and afternoon dates. Even if you *despise* the game of baseball, it's your contractual duty to teach this to your son. If you don't do it for you, do it for him. Same goes for throwing a tight spiral.

Swim. It's not necessary to be Michael Phelps, but if you can't even tread water, you risk getting saved from drowning by a woman or a child. Consider staying underwater.

MAXIM IN ACTION

Look at Shaquille O'Neal. Experts mostly agree: shooting a free throw underhanded—granny style—might actually *improve* Shaq's woeful free throw percentage. The Big Aristotle, however, knows that if he resorts to this ignominy, what he gains in percentages he loses in street cred, intimidation factor, and self-respect. The second he attempts a granny shot, he stops being the most feared player on the planet and starts being the biggest laughingstock since Shawn Bradley. If a 300-pound beast like *Shaq* can't get away with shooting a granny shot, then neither can you.

Figure 2.9. *This man should be shot.*

MAXIM EXCEPTIONS

If you're in a wheelchair you're off the hook, but you're still expected to compete in quadriplegic rugby. (Like Jason Street in *Friday Night Lights.*) Additionally, if you're clearly dominant in one sport, it gives you the luxury to slack off in others. If LeBron James played baseball, for instance, he could whiff every pitch and bat .025 and we wouldn't question his athleticism or virility. In fact, this has happened. His name was Michael Jordan.

MAXIM #20

ALWAYS BET ON ___.

WE LIVE IN a world where the World Series of Poker is shown on ESPN, so yes, this counts as a sport. (Barely.)

When you gamble, you have a theory. You always bet on ___, where "___" is some foolproof plan.

Right after college—broke and bulletproof—I whipped up a guaranteed scheme to win money at roulette. The idea was to keep betting on black (courtesy of Wesley Snipes from *Passenger 57*: "Always bet on black"), and then if you lose, you just bet *more* money on black, then repeat, then repeat until you're up. It can't fail. As long as you bet more than you're down—and you keep betting on black—mathematically you *must* win money.

MAXIM IN ACTION

Caesar's. Lake Tahoe. We get to the casino at 6 P.M., fresh-faced and sober. With only $337 in my checking account, I withdraw $100 from the ATM and plunk the whole bounty on black. The ball spins round and round . . . red. Dammit. No panic, no panic, I have a theory. I jog back to the ATM and withdraw $200. Again I put it all on black. The ball spins round and round . . . red. Huh. Now I'm down three bills.

So again I hit the ATM. Only four minutes have passed. I'm broke, but I cash-advance $300 with my credit card, which means getting fingerprinted by the cashier girl and filling out a packet of loser-loan papers. My buddies Jamie and Evan look at me in horror. I haven't even had one free drink. The dealer thinks I'm nuts. Already down $300, I take the three new hundred-dollar bills—which belong to MasterCard, technically—and put them all on black. The ball goes round and round. . . . Red.

Six minutes passed, $600 lost. This is more than I make in a week. Jamie throws an arm around my shoulder and says, "Hey man, let's go play some nickel slots." No. Not yet. I have a theory. I have a plan. The whole point is that you must *keep betting* on the same thing, so I cash advance $600 from my credit card, and the girl at the cashier's window—who just fingerprinted me—looks at me sadly, makes me fill out more loser-loan forms, and hands me a self-help brochure called "When the Fun Stops."

Back to the table. I'm down $600. I think about putting it on red. Red's hot, right? No, that's a sucker's move. There's no such thing as "hot" or "cold," that's a fallacy; the odds are all the same. I remember Wesley Snipes. I stick to my guns. I put the $600 on black. Since I'm playing at a low-stakes table—the old geezers are all betting $1 or $2—all eyes are on my bet. People betting on *red* wish me good luck. I feel like I'm in a Bond movie.

The ball goes round and round and round . . . lands on black!!!!! WHOO HOOO!!!!! And then bounces to red. Red 16.

So in the span of nine minutes, I lost $1,200.[1]

The moral of the maxim? You are not infallible. Your theories have weaknesses. And slavish adherence to some crazy plan without listening to your friends—whether in roulette, sports, relationships, parenting, or searching for WMDs—will get you a brochure called "When the Fun Stops."

MAXIM EXCEPTIONS

Maybe not an exception, per se, but a silver lining. I didn't actually lose $1,200. After that last fateful bet, Jamie and Evan dragged me to a club to cheer me up. The doorman said there was a $10 cover. Jamie told the guy that I just lost $1,200 in nine minutes, pleading for mercy. The doorman crossed his arms, considering. He looked at me, took in the sum total of my character. Finally he said, "I'll only charge him $5." See? A happy ending. I really only lost $1,195.

---

1. This isn't over. Caesar's only has my money *temporarily*. Someday I'll return with a $1,200 bet on black, and someday I'll break even. Even if it takes me a decade.

PART III.
WOMEN

MAXIM #21

USE EVERY FOUR-LETTER WORD BUT ONE.

IT STARTS WITH L, as in *Limiting your options*. It continues with O, as in *Oh shit*. Then V, as in *Valentine's-Day-gifts-and-related-horseshit*. It ends with E, as in *Eternity*—as in the fiery hell of forever.

You hate love. You refuse to say it before she does. And when she *does* say it, you squirm, you smile uncomfortably, and you brainstorm exit strategies. You're not ready to reciprocate, but you're trapped—you lack a viable comeback. That's because the comeback doesn't exist.

Pretend she just told you that she loves you for the very first time. Consider your options.

"Thank you." This is easily cracked code for "You suck. Please leave. This isn't working. It's not that I'm 'not attracted to you'; it's that you're unattractive. There's a difference. One's my fault; the other's yours. Goodbye now. Don't write. Or text. Or call. No, really. Goodbye. And thank you."

"I know." Only if you're about to get frozen in carbonite.

"I love the people you love." It just might perplex her for a few seconds, but soon she'll wise up and demand more. Even when delivered with panache and boyish charm, this is, at best, a Band-Aid.

"I find you really special." Only if you're gentleman enough to also give her a barf bag.

"You too." Still not great, but it's among the best of your bad options. It gives you wiggle room. It will flummox her, triggering a seven-hour debate among her girlfriends; they'll parse these two words, wondering what, exactly, you mean by "you too." A real head-scratcher. On the one hand, you didn't leave her hanging;

on the other, you didn't explicitly tell her that you love her. But you kind of implied it. Or did you?

My buddy Jamie had a theory. It was revolutionary. His idea was that the longer you wait, the more "I love you" is built up, the more it means, the deeper you get. Therefore, he postulated, it's best to drop the L-Bomb *early*—absurdly early—months before she expects it, thereby robbing the word of any meaning, any relevance, any power. It's like a pre-emptive strike. Premature emotive-ejaculation.

Hoping to keep things casual and avoid a serious relationship, he tried this once and only once. They're now married.

MAXIM IN ACTION

Let's examine some scenarios when you should *never* drop the L-Bomb.

Never tell her you love her as a means of apology.

Never tell her you love her so that she'll sleep with you. (You get sex, she gets scarred. Not cool.)

Never tell her you love her for the first time on Valentine's Day, then dump her that same day. Someone did that to my sister. And they still haven't found the body.

MAXIM EXCEPTIONS

When you've found "The One." (Little joke.) The only real exception is when you've exhausted all your escape routes, you've had your spirit broken, you've lost your will to fight. When you've been cornered, beaten, sapped of all your independence—then, and only then, it's time to profess your love. Because you're a romantic.

MAXIM #22

END THE CALL FIRST.

MEN CAN BE enlightened—take the phone, for instance. Just like pasteurization, TiVo, and the printing press, the phone is an important invention. The phone lets us order pizza. It lets us text message. It can be used in an emergency, like to call the cable company when the NBA League Pass isn't working.

The phone has many uses. One thing we frown upon, however, is use of the phone for talking. A quick call to coordinate plans? Not a problem. A brief, predinner chat to see if you want quiche or brisket? You bet. (Technically, in that scenario, we'd prefer a text. And come to think of it, the answer should be obvious: brisket.)

When you're on the phone with your girlfriend or wife, you must want to end the call before she does. To clarify, this doesn't mean that you, personally, must initiate the hang-up. Once again the key is *intent*. You mustn't be the blabberer.

On the call itself, your role is to silently suffer. Don't worry. You have plenty of options. You can flip the phone to mute and play video games or mow the lawn. You can utter a stream of "mmmh hmm," "that makes sense," or "exactly."

The advanced move? As you're checking your e-mail and surfing the web and utterly ignoring her, you say, "Right . . . but what do you *really* mean by that?" This sneaky little ace-in-the-hole, regardless of when you play it, yields unfailingly strong results. It conjures the illusion that you were not only paying close attention, but you're probing for something deeper. You're not just thinking about *what* she's saying, you're analyzing *why* she's saying it, you're assimilating this new information into a holistic, oft-analyzed view of her personality, and you want to know more. Try it sometime. It's good for the relationship.

MAXIM IN ACTION

Every group has one of these guys. When you're on a Vegas trip, he's the guy who leaves the blackjack table for "just a minute" to call his girlfriend, then returns an hour later, sheepish. This is the same guy who holds on 16.

Women say they want a man who's sensitive and communicative—fair enough. But they don't *really* want a guy who talks their earrings off. Ask questions. Don't soliloquize. Take a cue from George Costanza: end the conversation early and "leave 'em wanting more."

MAXIM EXCEPTIONS

Again, the phone itself is not evil. Phones don't bore; people do. And conversations themselves aren't necessarily awful. In fact, sometimes, a long conversation with a girl can be enjoyable. Really. (Preferably, this is done in person, which allows for the possibility of sex.)

So if there is truly, legit, honest-to-God news that's worth discussing at length, a thirty-plus-minute phone call is justified. If you're on business in Pittsburgh, say, and she calls to say she's pregnant, it's probably worth a leisurely chat.

MAXIM #23

ONLY FEAR ONE THING.

DEATH. GETTING OLD. Gonorrhea. These things don't scare you. There's only one little word that floods your heart with terror: commitment.

It doesn't matter if you're happy with the girl. You could be jubilant. You could be humping like jackrabbits, chafing from all the hot action, inventing new positions during the best sex of your life. With her, you never stop laughing. You love that she smells like strawberries. You think it's cute that she dips bagels into honey. You've never been happier. Ever. Yet the idea of *continuing* this happiness—of being as happy next month as you are today—strikes you as patently stupid.

Figure 3.3.
Kryptonite.

To clarify. You're actually able to commit to *some* things, just not women. In ascending order of importance, the things in this world that command your lifelong, undying commitment:

(1.) **Your old sneakers.** With torn laces and pancaked soles, they're not much good for anything besides mowing the lawn. Which is fine. They've done something that nothing—and no one—could ever do; they've spent their whole lives tolerating the odor of your feet. So they've earned your respect.

(2.) **Your old comic book collection.** If someone threatened to rob your old childhood house, steal your old Spider-Mans, then soak them with kerosene and light a match, your blood would boil over in rage. You'd never recover. If someone said that next week your girlfriend might move to London, you'd think, "I hope it's before Valentine's Day!" (See MAXIM #82.)

(3.) **Your favorite sports team**. (See MAXIM #11.)

51

(4.) **Your dog.** You don't think it's weird—because it's not—
that you refuse to promise your girlfriend a commitment
past Wednesday, but you're willing to pledge the next
nine, ten, fourteen years to a four-legged creature that
shits on your carpet.

(5.) **Your family.** If your brother gets arrested in Tijuana for
accidentally killing a hooker, you're on the next flight to
TJ and you'll bail him out, that old rascal.

MAXIM IN ACTION

Sadly, this maxim has become a cliché. The thing about clichés,
though, is that they're usually (in part, at least) true. I've gotten myself
into hot water—again and again—for telling girls that I'm afraid of
commitment. They think it's a line.

But it's not a line. It's not a gimmick. It's quite rational, really.
Whether they articulate it this way or not, guys wrestle with this fundamental issue: Why make a lifelong commitment based on a feeling of
caprice? People change. Unlike your shoes, dog, or comic books, the
girl can change—*you* can change. You'll commit when you positively
absolutely must. And not a moment sooner.

MAXIM EXCEPTIONS

Stripping the issue free of all the cheap jokes, why are we afraid
to make the commitment? Because it actually means something. We
don't take it lightly. So the exception to this maxim: once we actually
make the commitment, we honor it, we embrace it. The maxims of
manhood do not condone cheating.

(Is this paragraph an attempt to inoculate myself from future
attacks, or even provide a CYA to a future wife? That's crazy. What
would give you that idea? You've mistaken me for a cynic.)

MAXIM #24

SHE MUST BE HALF YOUR AGE, PLUS SEVEN.

SO LET'S CRUNCH the numbers. If you're 18, you're permitted to date a 16-year-old and no younger. When you hit 22, she better be old enough to vote. When you're 30, she needs to be 22—just old enough so you can't be suspected of meeting her at Parents' Weekend. When you're a bathrobe-wearing, leathery 90-year-old who hasn't had an erection since your second divorce, your new "girlfriend" must be 52. (I'm looking at you, Woody Allen.)

This age is the bare minimum. It is not, however, necessarily recommended. Sometimes, dating a much younger girl can trigger unforeseen complications. Believe it or not, after the first several dates and after you've had sex, in many cases, you'll begin to notice the girl's personality. You'll even start having conversations.

During the initial courtship phase, you see, these "conversations" are avoided through the workmanlike consumption of alcohol. True, you both say words, creating the illusion of a back-and-forth. But the chitchat is 60 percent flirting, 20 percent mindless blather, 12 percent lying, and a whopping 8 percent substance. Swap in "pandering" for "flirting" and it's the exact same ratio as a presidential debate.

MAXIM IN ACTION

Only after the third date, only after the dissipation of sexual tension, does the flirting subside and the actual conversation begin. At which point you begin to realize . . . this girl was born in a different decade. This girl doesn't remember a time before Facebook. This girl has never seen a floppy disk. When you make a reference to *Harold and Kumar*, she laughs and says the she loves all the "old classics."

When you text back and forth, you can't quite follow her acronyms. Sure, LOL is straightforward enough, but WYCM? You ask her what it means, she tells you Will You Call Me and laughs at your "oldmanishness," then tells you don't worry about it because NALOPKT. Huh? Not a Lot of People Know That. Actually, they do. But none of them were born before 1993.

Your dates begin to feel different. At first, you both like to go to the same bars and the same clubs, then you realize that you no longer like "going to clubs"—you outgrew that years ago—and you have absolutely no desire to dance (see MAXIM #61). She wants to do shots, and while you certainly *could* do shots (see MAXIM #63), you'd rather enjoy a good night of sex and then a good night of sleep.

Then you both have another drink, and all is well again. For now.

MAXIM EXCEPTIONS

Like Newtonian physics, this rule unravels at the subatomic level. If you're an 8-year-old munchkin, technically, this means that you can't date any girls younger than 11. Which is weird. The maxim, therefore, goes into effect the second you blow out the candles at your sixteenth birthday party.

"WEDDING PLANNING" MEANS PLANNING TO PROBABLY SHOW UP.

YOU'RE NOT CATEGORICALLY opposed to weddings. They have merit. Weddings serve important functions: getting your friends drunk, stuffing your attic with china, and ensuring your girlfriend stays nice and skinny.

So you tolerate the wedding. You humor your fiancée. You smile and nod as she flips through magazines like *Modern Bride* and *Wedding Cake Weekly.* New glossy issues—you call it your bride's "wedding porn"—arrive in the mail every day, cluttering your living room. And that's all fine. You roll with it.

But when the chips are down, you can tell the difference between toleration and participation. You won't actively *sabotage* her planning, per se, but you won't turn into Martin Short in *Father of the Bride.* You may not take the lead.

Figure 3.5.
Bow and arrow.

MAXIM IN ACTION

It is unacceptable for you to say anything remotely like: "Honey? Have a sec? This is important. For the table decorations, my buddy Jason suggested a nice bouquet of tulips, since they'll go swimmingly with the lavender bridesmaid dresses."

This statement is wrong in fifty-three ways.

For starters, you shouldn't know about tulips. You shouldn't know that they're lavender. (Are they? I refuse to fact-check.) You shouldn't use the word "lavender" (unless it's the name of a stripper) or even know that it's a color (see MAXIM #2).

And why are you and Jason talking about flowers? Was it during your mud bath? You both should be strapped to a couch and forced to watch twenty-four consecutive hours of looped *Rambo: First Blood.*

Still more problems. "Swimmingly" is a word that may never leave your lips. You shouldn't be aware of any need for "table decorations." You've stopped caring about "bridesmaid dresses" now that you'll never take one off a girl again.

The biggest violation? This issue is not "important." To clarify, this doesn't mean that your fiancée is not important. It doesn't mean that your marriage, your future, your oath of commitment is unimportant. That stuff matters. In fact . . . you view this ceremony as so solemn, so special that the last thing you want to do is lose focus by getting mired in the trivial details. Your undying love is important. Table decorations are not. (Good luck with this argument; 7 percent of the time it works 100 percent of the time.)

MAXIM EXCEPTIONS

There are three components of the wedding that demand your involvement.

(1.) **Family guest-list politics.** Negotiating the invite list is only slightly less polemical than carving up Jerusalem or bringing playoffs to college football. It's not fair to dump it on your fiancée: step up to bat.

(2.) **The alcohol at the reception.** You should ensure that the booze you want will be available and plentiful.

(3.) **The music.** This is your one chance to dodge schmaltziness. Seize it.

MAXIM #26

NEVER ASK FOR HER NUMBER.

YOU'RE SCRATCHING YOUR head. Huh? "Isn't that the *point* of talking to girls in bars? Isn't that the glorious meme of *Swingers*, getting numbers, getting digits?"

There's a better way. When you say to a girl, "Can I have your number?" you give her the chance to say *no*. Never give her that window. Follow these seven steps:

(1.) Give her your card. (You do have business cards on hand, right? Good.)
(2.) Take a second card from your wallet.
(3.) Flip the second card over, blank side up.
(4.) Grab a pen.
(5.) Hold the pen over the card like you're getting ready to write.
(6.) Ask her, "What's the best way to reach you, phone or e-mail?"
(7.) Check. Mate.

That's just part of your bag of tricks. Other tactics you should (and probably already do) follow include:

Eye contact. A little obvious? Perhaps. But like keeping your head down when swinging a golf club, it's something simple and basic that's easy to forget. Strong eye contact is more important than what you say, especially if you're dumb.

Don't use a line. Unless delivered with extraordinary humor and panache (I have neither), a pickup line is embarrassing for all parties involved. You don't need to say anything witty, even. You'll be surprised by the mileage a simple "How's it going" will get you.

A picture's worth a thousand whores. A group of girls, once they've consumed at least three sips of alcohol, is physically incapable of going an hour without pictures. This is a layup. Just volunteer to take their picture, tell them it came out great ("that's a framer!"), and you're instantly involved in their conversation. This is also a proven tactic for being the wedge (see MAXIM #81).

MAXIM IN ACTION

My buddy Wes called it the "Confidence Theory." Out of all a guy's attributes—looks, humor, money, intelligence, career cachet, height, fashion sense, odor—confidence trumps the entire list. A confident troll will get more action than the insecure prince. And how do you *get* more confidence? Think of it like weightlifting. When you go to the gym for the very first time, you're not going to be able to bench-press 300 pounds. You start with the barbell. Then you add 10 pounds, 20, 30, and soon you're pumping a stack of plates. Apply this principle to girls. If you're super shy and don't have much confidence, hit on a girl who's emphatically *less good-looking than you*. Get her number (without asking for it, obviously). Next time, try someone a little less pudgy, then a girl who's almost cute, then a girl you'll actually want to call. Like making sausage, the process of romance isn't pretty.

MAXIM EXCEPTIONS

If it's in the bag, it's in the bag. Let's say you meet the girl at nine o'clock at the bar, you hit it off, you've bought each other a couple rounds of drinks, and you chat and flirt until midnight, ignoring your respective huddles of friends. You've already had a de facto first date, so at the end of the night, there's very little risk in asking for her number, straight up. Then again . . . why take chances?

ALWAYS HOLD THE DOOR.

YOU HOLD THE door for her. Period. Whether it's a car door, hotel door, restaurant door, or train door, and even—brace yourself—whether she's cute or gross, young or old, single or taken, model or troll. It's not about scoring points. It's about chivalry.

Other required acts of chivalry:

Light her cigarette. I'm not a smoker. I don't have any philosophical problems with cigarettes—any industry that creates jobs, keeps our doctors busy, and gives something to the kiddos is okay by me—but I've never enjoyed the taste. Many years ago, back in my embarrassing early days of flirting, I leaned in to light a girl's cigarette. I had two problems. First, I couldn't operate the lighter. Literally—I didn't know how to make it work. (It was my first time.) Second, and even more humiliating, I lit the wrong end of her cigarette. It's very, very difficult to come off as a suave lothario when she's laughing at your incompetence.

Hail her a cab. No, you don't have to do one of those freakily high-pitched cab whistles, but you must follow one principle: be bold. You should actively put your body in the street (leaving the sidewalk) and aggressively stare down a cab. Decisiveness matters. Of course, helplessly watching fifty-eight occupied cabs zip past isn't quite Cary Grant, either, so keep a car service number in your cell as backup.

Help her with her coat. If it's one of those fitted little "girl sweaters" that's smaller than your boxers, forget it. But if it's an actual coat-coat, the kind of thing she wears when cold? Help her in; help her out.

Carry her heavy objects. If she's lugging anything more burdensome than a dictionary, ask if you can carry it. You're not implying she's a weakling; you're just being a gentleman.

Advanced move: Pull out her chair. This one can be tricky. It's not always welcome, it's not always feasible, and it just might lead to you ramming her breasts into the table. Which is less sexy than it sounds.

MAXIM IN ACTION

It's a cliché: everyone moans that "chivalry is dead." Fine. The question, though, is when? Take this quote:

"The age of chivalry has gone; the age of humanity has come."

Post-feminist rants in 2008? Nope, Charles Sumner in the nineteenth century. Or:

"But the age of chivalry is gone. That of sophists, economists, and calculators, has succeeded; and the glory of Europe is extinguished forever."

Courtesy of Edmund Burke, 1790. Or this one:

"The age of chivalry is past. Bores have succeeded to dragons."

From Charles Dickens. The point? Ninety years from now, people will sigh and say, "Oh, chivalry is dead! It's not like it was back in the good old 2010s." Chivalry isn't an *era* that lives or dies. It starts with you and ends with you. Make of it what you will.

MAXIM EXCEPTIONS

This old debate bores me, and I suspect it bores you, too, so we'll keep this brief. Is there a sinister, underlying presumption in chivalry that women *need* help from men—implying they're weaker, incapable of helping themselves—which therefore makes it sexist? It's a fair question. You shouldn't be condescending or overbearing. Assuming you're neither, the next time she brings this up, just ask her to get the door and carry your suitcase.

MAXIM #28

GO FOR RBIs, NOT BATTING AVERAGE.

THERE'S THE OLD saying about a guy who walks into a bar and asks every woman he sees, "Excuse me, may I jump your bones?" And 99 times out of 100, he gets kneed in the balls or soaked with beer. But that 1 time out of the 100—that's something special, that's something magical.

The key to meeting women is not giving a shit. You need to be loose, fearless, and unsaddled by expectations. You don't fear rejection. You embrace it. When you worry about your batting average, you choke.

Once you get comfortable with failure—wallow in it—you prime yourself for success. Yes, this smacks of cliché, but it merits discussion nonetheless: you have absolutely *nothing to lose*. As reductive as this sounds, let's consider the possible consequences of hitting on a random girl in the bar.

Scenario 1: She's into you. The two of you laugh, flirt, touch forearms, exchange numbers. Good work.

Scenario 2: She's not feeling it. As you awkwardly sip your empty beer and fumble through stilted conversation, she nervously glances back at her friends with a "help" look in her eyes, then she whips out her cell phone and has a sudden, urgent need to text her cousin. Okay. Dead end. But here's the thing . . . who cares? You've known this girl for less than thirty seconds. You'll never see her again. Unless you did something wretched like the guy above (the bone-jumper), she won't say anything toxic to her friends. Relax. Focus on the positive: that's one less girl who might give you a disease.

Scenario 3: She's booze-hooking. A booze-hooker trolls the bar for free drinks, accepts your cocktail, flirts for five minutes, then pivots away. Because you never know which girls are booze-hookers (they blend in), never buy drinks as a shortcut for an introduction. You want the girl to like you on your own merits, not because you're bribing her with liquor.

MAXIM IN ACTION

Years ago my friend Wes—who gets credit (and blame) for most of my theories on dating and flirting—called it "first blood." When you go out on Friday night with your buddies, you'll start a little stiff, a little anxious, a little nervous. But once you draw first blood—once you hit on the first group of girls—you immediately relax and get into a groove. It could be a flop. It could end in twelve seconds. She could turn away without even saying hello. It doesn't matter. Half the battle is drawing first blood: after that, you'll feel more comfortable the rest of the night. Try it.

MAXIM EXCEPTIONS

All of the above applies to random girls at bars, coffee shops, laundromats, and trains (see MAXIM #89). The advice does *not* apply to girls you know through friends. These demand more tact. For girls whom you might actually see again, forget RBIs. What counts is not getting an Error.

MAXIM #29

KEEP THE ONE-NIGHT-STANDS CLASSY.

A LITTLE CASUAL sex never hurt anyone. (Except for when it poisons friendships, or leads to emotional scarring, or explodes into political scandal, or triggers the breakup of the band, or ends a marriage, or leads to an unwanted pregnancy, or infects someone with an STD and kills them, or—if you're so inclined—damns your soul to an eternity of pain, fire, and unrelenting torture. Other than all that, a little casual sex never hurt anyone.)

Casual sex is just one more plank of the sexual revolution—a natural extension of feminism, really—so you're honoring the principles of women's suffrage, Betty Friedan, Virginia Woolf, Gandhi, and Betty Crocker. Flings are fine. You may not, however, act like a douchebag.

Specifically, you may never be the following:

The Bait-and-Switcher. You may not pretend to really, *really* be into her—hinting that you want a serious relationship, you want her as a girlfriend—and then give her the pink slip, without two-week's notice, as soon as you dip your stick.

Figure 3.9.
Inner-sanctum.

The Fader-Outer. You may not make plans and then cancel, and then make even vaguer, out-there-in-the-future plans and cancel, then gradually space out the plans for weeks and weeks, teasing and taunting her because you lack the balls to end it. Suck it up. Rip the Band-Aid.

The Taker. Don't be that guy who doesn't know how to reciprocate. It doesn't matter if you never see each other again: if you receive, give.

The Creepy Aggressor. True, guys never want to take it slow (see MAXIM #30). But that absolutely does not give you license to keep pushing, pushing, pushing until she's uncomfortable and borderline scared. Gross. Wrong.

The Poorly Disguised Regretter. Maybe she looks worse in the morning. (So do you, buddy.) Keep that to yourself. You can feel it, but you can't betray any hint of buyers' remorse. Keep your game face on.

MAXIM IN ACTION

I used to date a girl named Cain Girl. At around 2 A.M. on the night we met (at a bar named Cain), she said that she forgot her keys and didn't have a place to sleep—could I help her out? I'm a gentleman, so of course I volunteered my services. The first night we hooked up, Cain Girl threw me against a wall and asked what I wanted as a "safety word." I was so flummoxed (and drunk) that I said the first thing that popped in my head, the lamest, least original word imaginable: Uncle. (I'm still blushing.) As for any emotions, any douchebaggery? After several more hookups—which never once involved a substantive conversation, dinner, or even proper phone call—I get a drunken text from Cain Girl at 4:47 A.M. on a Tuesday. (Tuesday!) The text, literally word for word without any embellishment: "Any chance you're still out and want to fuck?" Which leads to . . .

MAXIM EXCEPTIONS

Technically there's no exception that permits you to be a douchebag, but some relationships are so casual, so clearly just about the booty, that you needn't walk on emotional eggshells. Anything goes. In the case of Cain Girl, me being the Fader-Outer would be perfectly acceptable. She was The Player. In cases like Cain Girl, you can walk away with a clear conscience. And in this case, she walked away from me. Afterward, my buddy Stephane told me something I hadn't considered: "You do realize that the text message—'Any chance you're still out and want to fuck?'—went to multiple recipients, right?"

MAXIM #30

DON'T TAKE THINGS SLOW.

WE PLAY ALONG. When backed into a corner, we agree that sure, *absolutely*, let's "take things slow" and not rush into anything too physical, too soon.

We're lying. Always. No guy in history has ever actually wanted to take things slow. In fact, we always want 20 percent more than what's on the table, regardless of what's being offered. It's never enough.

If the first date ends with a humiliating peck on the cheek, we long for—and think we'd be satisfied with—a simple brushing of the lips and maybe a flicker of tongue. That's all we want. If we get tongue? Suddenly it's not enough, and our heart's set on a marathon make-out session; that'd be plenty, really, just a long deep kiss. Then our thirst would be quenched.

Like a meth addict who can never get a strong enough hit, still we want more. Only a make-out session on the first date? Please, making-out's for junior high, we want a hand-job. But if we get one of those . . . only a hand-job, *really*? We have hands.

If the first date ends with oral sex? It could be off the charts, but even now, even as we approach the promised land, a sliver of our consciousness thinks, "Hmmm, did I bring a condom, where can I get a condom, we need to have sex—actual sex, intercourse sex—if we don't have sex-sex, this date's a complete failure." (Note to all past and present and future dates: this doesn't apply to you.)

MAXIM IN ACTION

We're so focused on sex, so focused on pushing the limits as far as they can be (reasonably, responsibly, noncreepily) pushed, that at times we get a little confused. One night at 3 A.M., postcoital, during pillow talk, the girl whispered in my ear, hot and breathy, "Do you want to pee with me?" Huh. No, not really, thanks. I'd never had a hankering to try a golden shower. But what the hell, I'm not a prude. So I try and be a good sport. Without saying a word, I take her hand and we walk from my bedroom to the bathroom. Neither one of us speaks. How does this whole golden shower operation work, exactly? Does she simply want me to watch her pee? Okay, I'll do it. So she sits on the toilet—looks at me with an expression I can't decipher—and starts to pee. We kiss some. It's unsexy and awkward. We fool around for a while, wash our hands extra thoroughly, then return to the bedroom. Only hours later did I realize that she was, in fact, trying to inquire about the state of our relationship, and what she actually whispered was, "Do you want to *be* with me?" To which I responded by dragging her to the bathroom and watching her urinate. Now that's romance.

MAXIM EXCEPTIONS

You already know this and I already know this—everyone should already know this—but it never hurts to repeat: No means no, not-tonight means no, I'm-not-comfortable means no, fuck-off means no, and I'll call the cops or kick you in the balls means no. There's a fine line between acting bold and acting like a creep. Don't come near this line.

PART IV.
HEALTH AND FOOD

MAXIM #31

KNOW HOW TO MAKE
A KILLER BREAKFAST.

HERE'S HOW YOU "cook" lunch: you whip out a loaf of bread, you
glob on some mustard, and then you stuff the fucker with ham and
turkey. And that's that. Sometimes, if you're feeling daring, you might
garnish the entrée with potato chips.

For dinner? You have six options:

(1.) **Cook pasta.** When you're feeling truly up to a culinary
challenge, you bust open the package of spaghetti and
crack a bottle of Prego. Seven times out of ten, you're
blazingly competent at boiling water and nuking the
sauce. Luckily you were born with a tolerance for endless
repetition, so you don't mind the same meal cooked the
same way for the entirety of your twenties.

(2.) **Grill** (see MAXIM #34).

(3.) **Make Hamburger Helper.** You can smell a bargain, and this
is the best one since Ramen. When you're truly broke, you
have no qualms about skipping the hamburger. Cousin
Eddie said it best in *National Lampoon's Vacation*: "I don't
know why they call this stuff Hamburger Helper. It does
just fine by itself."

(4.) **Order delivery.** In a little cabinet next to your coffee table,
you have a drawer with your most valuable possessions:
157 take-out menus, many of which are identical copies
that the delivery dude keeps slapping on your front door.
This drawer keeps you fed. This drawer has saved your life.

(5.) **Microwave dinners.** You're damn right; this counts as
cooking. The button doesn't press itself.

(6.) **Reheat the leftovers from Option 1.**

This is all just preamble for a maxim that's more important than you might think: while your lunch and dinner skills in the kitchen are worse than Buddy's in *Elf* ("Maple Syrup!"), you must know how to make a four-star breakfast.

It's not for you. It's for her. The guy who can conjure up Belgian waffles, brew a perfect pot of coffee, and serve it with fresh blueberries—this is the guy who gets repeat business. This is the guy she remembers. Even if you never see her again, breakfast ends the date with class.

MAXIM IN ACTION

You only need a few go-to moves. In fact, it doesn't matter if you only have *one* killer recipe—it's a new meal for every new girl. Rochelle Bilow of the blog "SexyGirlsEat" tells us, "Do something sweet, not savory. No girl wants to eat a three-egg omelet with a guy right after she just . . . you know. Go with pancakes, Belgian waffles, or yogurt with honey. If you make pancakes, instead of using syrup, impress her with crème fraîche. Top them with fruit. This way the girl will think it's more healthy and counteracts the pancakes." Which fruit should you serve her? "Not strawberries—too cliché. Not cantaloupe—too much like a hotel's continental breakfast. Go with fresh blueberries or blackberries."

MAXIM EXCEPTIONS

While it's mandatory that you know how to make her a divine breakfast, it's not mandatory that you actually do it. You'll have many awkward, drunken hookups that end in the shared confusion of morning, with both of you asking, "Who are you, and why are you buck naked in my bed?" In these groggy moments of intimacy, the last thing either of you wants is to slurp down a platter of eggs. Then again, ask her. You'd be surprised. After you've had sex with a stranger, breakfast can serve as a fine introduction.

MAXIM #32

COUNT PROTEIN, NOT CALORIES.

COUNTING CALORIES IS for girls. You're not even sure that calories *exist*, actually. They're probably like the "ether," that mysterious substance that scientists thought permeated the universe and explained all of physics. Then, in 1879, Albert Michelson conducted an experiment and concluded (paraphrased): "Oh, fuck! There's no ether. For the past two thousand years, we kinda sorta blew it. It doesn't exist at all."

If they were wrong about ether, maybe they're wrong about calories. So you don't count them. It's vain. It's superficial. You do, however, believe in a methodical study of your daily intake of protein. You set targets. You create a table in Excel. You google "how to bulk up" and you discover esoteric metrics like the "protein quotient." You calculate that to get ripped—shredded—you need 180 grams a day.

You take stock of your current intake: 4 grams from cereal in the morning, 15 grams from lunch, etc., etc., and that gives you a grand total of . . . 47. Huh.

So you overhaul your entire diet. In the mornings you wolf down three hardboiled eggs. Every meal has a slab of chicken breast; you toss chicken into pasta, rice, salad, tomato soup.

And tuna. You gobble up tuna. It's cheap and rich with protein (35 grams per serving!), so you pop two cans a day. Your breath is chronically foul. And still, through all of this, you silently snicker at how obsessed your girlfriend is about her weight.

After this diet metamorphosis, you do the math and tabulate the new total . . . 113 grams. Shit. 113? That's it? After all that? So you take the final plunge: you go to GNC and buy those tubs of chocolate protein powder. (You don't precisely know what "whey" is and you don't want to know.)

At last. You've done it. You're now at 180 grams. Sure, you have to interrupt your routine every forty-five minutes to eat a "snack" that makes you want to vomit. True, you're dropping an extra $200 a week.

Yes, you're now spending an alarming amount of time on the crapper. But the important thing—the only thing—is that you're not the weirdo who gets a low-fat muffin.

MAXIM IN ACTION

At 23 I was scrawny. So I went through a bulk-up protein phase that employed the following ten-step diet:

(1.) Two packs of oatmeal
(2.) Weight-gainer shake
(3.) Gym
(4.) A second breakfast with eggs, toast, bacon, homefries
(5.) Can of tuna (straight from the can, no mayo)
(6.) Lunch with an extra-large ham sandwich
(7.) Second weight-gainer shake
(8.) Second can of tuna (again, straight from the can—I ate this at my desk, coworkers loved the smell)
(9.) A sensible dinner
(10.) A third weight-gainer shake just before bed

This lasted for three months. I gained twenty-five pounds . . . and I'm still trying to lose it.

MAXIM EXCEPTIONS

If you're fat, you're fat. No one will mock you for counting calories. What's not permitted, however, is a skinny-to-average-to-slightly-paunchy dude obsessing over whether he's allotted 240 or 270 calories before lunch. As explained earlier, men are never body-image conscious.

MAXIM #33

NO CLASSES AT THE GYM.

BARBELLS. DUMBELLS. THE BENCH. THE TREADMILL. That's it. That's the list of authorized gym equipment. No giant rubber bouncy balls that look like they've been stolen from Willy Wonka's chocolate factory. No thigh masters. And above all else, your trip to the gym may not involve a class.

You're not quite sure what happens in these so-called classes, but they seem to include lots of spandex, lots of pink, and lots of women writhing on the floor like they're auditioning for a Christina Aguilera video.

You view these classes with deep suspicion, lumping them in the same category as cricket, ska music, and imported cheese that doesn't need refrigeration. The one thing you know is that each class has only one guy. And it's not you.

Five classes you want no part of:

(1.) **Cardio Kickboxing.** You like the idea of kicking something . . . as long as it's to crack a dude's ribs or bust down a door. Granted, if you were in Will Ferrell's truth tree (the one in *Old School* with the little birds), you'd concede that you've never actually kicked anyone—much less broken down a door—but you understand, instinctively, that kicks are reserved for violence and bloodshed, not opening up chakras.

(2.) **Pilates.** No man's exercise should focus on "centering." It shouldn't be about your core. Exercise must involve powerful, brutish, injury-inducing motions that build raw muscle. You might be tempted to infiltrate the women's class so you can be that "sensitive guy." Good idea. Here's a better one: pretend to use the same gynecologist.

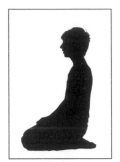

Figure 4.3. *Never play a sport that you can't win.*

(3.) **Yoga.** (See MAXIM #36.)

(4.) **Step Aerobics.** Like Rocky, you frown on precise, sophisticated training that can just as easily be performed outdoors. If you want to climb steps, you'll sprint up and down the bleachers, dammit. If it gives you pneumonia or shatters your ankle, so be it. Better to get fat and injured honorably than get trim, healthy, and attractive the wrong way.

(5.) **Pole dancing.** No.

MAXIM IN ACTION

It always begins the same way. You're having trouble hitting the gym on a regular basis ("regular" meaning more than twice a baseball season) and your buddy tells you about this awesome class that toned his abs, dropped his weight, and ripped his delts. You're intrigued. You remember what it was like to have abs, all those many years ago. You're not quite sure where your delts are, but you know they could be a little bigger. So you go for it.

Once you're in, you're in. Soon you're signing up for "Abs boot camp" (boot camp is for the Army, Navy, Marines, and nothing else) and "Jazz Aerobics." You drink wheat-germ shakes. You start matching your workout tops and bottoms. (You've long since stopped calling them shirts and shorts.) And none of this strikes you as weird.

MAXIM EXCEPTIONS

This is a gray area and somewhat controversial, but you are allowed to join a cycling class. True, it's better to do this alone—on a real bike on a real road—but if you absolutely must take a gym class, you may save face in this torture chamber. Why's this different? Because there's nothing patronizing or emasculating or gimmicky about it: the goal is to sweat. And sweat and sweat until you're Ted Striker from *Airplane!*

MAXIM #34

MAN THE GRILL.

YOU'RE AS COMPETENT with the grill as you are incompetent with the oven. You can't explain it. Roasting a turkey is for those who happen to own a pair of breasts; grilling a steak is for those who happen to own a pair of testicles. Fair? Sensible? Irrelevant. This is the way you grew up. It's the way your children will grow up. "Irrationality" is no reason to abandon tradition: just look at the metric system, Santa, and the electoral college.

You follow these five rules of the grill:

(1.) At a barbecue, you log more grill time than your wife. This isn't to say that she's never allowed to grill. That's just sexist. However, just like with a rental car, she may not be the primary griller. If she's on the burgers and you're tossing the salad, you might as well wear a floral apron saying "Kiss the Cook!" while sipping a wine cooler.

(2.) Like a pitcher, you can start, give middle relief, and close. Let's say, you're at a buddy's barbecue. If he's manning the grill and has to take a leak—the only reason he'd leave his post—when he hands you the tongs, you're able to step right in, flip the dogs, and avoid dropping meat into the charcoal.

(3.) You also know *not* to interfere with another man's grill unless asked. You can't give advice. You can't complain. You can't say, "How about we add some curry powder?" And no, you can't even say, "I think you should take 'em off now." That's his call, not yours. Your friend is giving you food. In exchange, you will risk salmonella.

(4.) You keep your grill as clean as your whistle. Your closet, garage, and bedroom could look like the post-apocalyptic wasteland in *28 Days Later*. Maybe you're a slob. Your grill, however, is clean enough to, um, eat off.

(5.) You own the right tools. This is the one category of kitchen supplies where you refuse to cut corners. Nothing fires you up like getting a new Weber basting brush, spatula, or locking tongs. You'd like to buy the new $160 set of stainless steel skewers, but your wife has foolishly squandered the budget on basic plates and silverware.

MAXIM IN ACTION

The griller is a warrior. He just does his thing. He plugs away and flips the steaks, sipping beer, focused on the meat so he doesn't have to listen to his wife. His buddies, however, are charged with one obligation: they need to keep him company. If the griller is outside while the party's indoors, at least two friends should huddle by the grill, ping-ponging their conversation between sports and stories of nostalgia, trying, for this one fleeting afternoon, to resurrect a golden era of youth and simplicity.

MAXIM EXCEPTIONS

If you live in a small apartment that has no room for a grill, yes, this buys you a little leeway, but you're not off the hook. Keep your skills sharp. Whenever you go home to visit your folks, squeeze in a few practice sessions on Dad's grill. It'll make him happy, and years from now when you finally have your own place, it'll keep you away from the wine coolers.

MAXIM #35

ORDER FOOD THAT'S SIMPLER, LARGER, AND FATTIER THAN THE GIRL'S.

MEN EAT BURGERS. Steaks. Bloody slabs of rib eye. The ability to chew, digest, and savor dead animals isn't just delicious and nourishing —it's what separates us from goldfish.

Feasting on red meat, fat, and heaping platters of carbs is what keeps our species going. It's primordial. It's in our bones. Regardless of whom you're dining with, you must order the juiciest, manliest meal within your budget.

And if you're on a date? You are absolutely forbidden from ordering a wimpy meal. If you order the Honey Lime Fruit Salad (with dressing on the side) and she orders the Black Angus Steak, you've surrendered both your manhood and any chance of sex.

Progressive minds might argue, "Isn't counting calories sensible? Wouldn't it keep you in better shape, improve your nutrition, and make you even more attractive to women?"

They don't get it. True, fitness matters (see MAXIM #32). Clearly, though, the only logical way to stay in shape is by lifting so much weight that you

Figure 4.5.
A light lunch.

almost (but not quite) cripple your back, and running so many miles that you *almost* (but not quite) shred your knees. You look good by sweating and bleeding. Not dieting.

She can be fussy. You can't. She might request extra walnuts or balsamic vinegar, but you will order the #3, period. No substitutions. No swapping the 2 percent for fat-free milk. Your stomach can handle anything; it's further evidence of your vitality.

There's also a very real social dynamic at play. To make a sweeping generalization (my first), women will be uncomfortable, even peeved, if you order a dainty salad and they get a bucket of nachos. You've not only emasculated yourself, you've tilted the natural harmony of food, making *her*, by contrast, feel less feminine. In other words, you're not just a sissy. You're rude.

MAXIM IN ACTION

Blame Meg Ryan and Billy Crystal. At one point Sally says, "I'd like the chef salad please with the oil and vinegar on the side. And the apple pie à la mode. . . . But I'd like the pie heated, and I don't want the ice cream on top, I want it on the side. And I'd like strawberry instead of vanilla if you have it. If not, then no ice cream, just whipped cream, but only if it's real. If it's out of a can, then nothing."

If Harry had been the one ordering this meal, Sally would have stalked out of the restaurant in disappointment, ending the movie right then and there.

MAXIM EXCEPTIONS

If you're allergic to a particular ingredient, you are permitted to request its removal. You are also allowed to order extra gravy or extra butter; the principle of fattiness offsets the principle of simplicity. If you've already eaten a heroic portion of food—a late lunch, say—you are permitted to order something light. And if you're truly obese—as in you're the group's fat-comic-relief friend—please order the salad.

MAXIM #36

YOU DON'T TRUST THIS "YOGA."

SPIRITUAL ENLIGHTENMENT? INNER peace? Harmony? If it belongs in a fortune cookie, it doesn't belong in the gym. You don't trust yoga for the following eleven reasons:

The uniforms. You're not wearing capris. Ever. The fact that yoga pants are looser, more comfortable, and less leotard-like than football tights is irrelevant.

The chakras. You're not precisely sure what "chakras" are, but you're confident you don't want any. That's why you wear a condom.

The positions. You think you saw reenactments of the Standing Forward Bend, Downward Facing Dog, and Legs-up-the-Wall on a season finale of *Oz*. If it could happen in the prison laundry room, it shouldn't happen in the gym.

The passivity. Yoga teaches patience and reflection, two virtues now unnecessary thanks to iPhones and BlackBerries.

The mats. You could walk around town with a purple yoga mat slung over your shoulder. You could also walk around in a tutu. Six of one, half a dozen . . .

The lack of exercise. Sorry. It just doesn't add up. Sitting perfectly still for ninety minutes doesn't count as real exercise. The fact that everyone in the room (including the men) looks lean, fit, and more attractive than you is irrelevant.

The side effects. Yoga claims to reduce your overall level of hostility. This may or may not be true, but either way it's not worth finding out.

The flexibility. The ability to put your legs behind your head is something that you never, ever want to use.

The awkward relaxation issue. You've seen what happens when you "relax" certain muscles in your tailbone. And gyms don't come with bathroom vents.

The noncompetitiveness. Every sport has competition, a villain, a way to keep score. You'll get curious as soon as they find a way to pit the ying against the yang.

The pride. You're pretty sure that your girlfriend is a better yoga-er than you, so it's better to stick to sports with an even playing field. Like weightlifting.

MAXIM IN ACTION

Unfortunately for fans of the Miami Dolphins, the *Maxims of Manhood* was not published in 2004. That's the year Ricky Williams "retired" from the NFL at the ripe old age of 26 to pursue a career of smoking pot, traveling through Asia, studying holistic medicine, and swapping his shoulder pads for a yoga mat. It's the most public castration since Lorena Bobbit or Michael Jackson.

MAXIM EXCEPTIONS

If you actually live in India, Tibet, or a culture that raised you to practice yoga, ignore this chapter and mock my ignorance. Tradition is important. Honoring your culture is important. But if you grew up between the 68th and 120th longitudes, not working out like Richard Simmons is also important.

MAXIM #37

NO STRAWS, CHERRIES, OR UMBRELLAS.

TRUE STORY. BACK in college, when I was visiting home for the holidays, one night my mom took me to a Mexican restaurant. The waiter asked for our orders. I wasn't yet twenty-one, but I ordered chicken fajitas and a watermelon margarita.

My mom looked at me. She shook her head.

"Oh, I know I'm not twenty-one," I stammered, "But I thought, you know, maybe since I'll be turning twenty-one in a few months . . ." My mom said that she had no problem with me ordering alcohol, but if I'm getting a drink, it had better be a beer. She didn't want me to turn out like Judge Reinhold's character in *Beverly Hills Cop*, the goofy guy who ordered a Smurf-blue cocktail with a crazy straw and bushel of fruit.

To this day, I owe my lifelong appreciation of beer to my mother. It's one of her enduring lessons. And Mom was right. Acceptable drinks include beer, wine, select cocktails, and liquor. That doesn't mean you can't mix it up, add variety. Ordering champagne— especially when unexpected—adds panache to any random Tuesday.

Figure 4.7. *Don't embarrass Mom.*

The art of ordering the right mixed drink is a broader topic (look for it in the sequel), but some quick rules of thumb: it shouldn't include milk (no white Russians), shouldn't require a blender, and if you order a mimosa for brunch, hold the OJ and don't call it a mimosa.

MAXIM IN ACTION

You're on a date. She orders a dark, creamy, chocolaty "mocha martini" sprinkled with drops of caramel. Let's not bullshit ourselves. It looks good. It looks delicious. It looks like the best dessert you've ever had crossed with premium liquor crossed with pangs of childhood nostalgia. If sex were served in a glass, it would look like this. You're tempted . . .

Snap out of it. Yes, she's ordering a heavenly drink. You know what? She's also wearing a purse. The moment you break that seal—ordering this milky slice of perfection—is the moment you think, "Huh. That purse she has . . . it's not a bad idea. It's a good place to store my keys, my cell, my wallet . . . and it would even match my shoes."

She gets the purse. She gets the mocha martini. You get the cumulative benefits of 10,000+ years of gender inequities. Call it a wash.

MAXIM EXCEPTIONS

When you vacation somewhere with oceans, hammocks, gleaming white beaches, and a bubble of tropical paradise, it's not only permissible to order a fruity and otherwise off-limits drink, it's compulsory. Everything has its time and place. (Except long white socks.)

Another loophole. Some restaurants and lounges stake their reputation on a particular drink or theme. Assuming this theme isn't Planet Hollywood, you are permitted to indulge. Let's say, for example, you're on a date at a swanky mojito lounge in South Beach. Even Mom would let you try the mojitos.

MAXIM #38

AVOID BOTH PEDICURES
AND TOE FUNGUS.

NO MANICURES. NO man makeup. That's all covered in MAXIM #41. But there's one troublesome corollary: in this new era of sex and dating, when you get naked with a woman, she now has certain expectations about personal hygiene. It's no longer enough that you have a penis. You must conform to a new standard.

She expects you to do the following:

Clip your toenails. Toe fungus isn't sexy. Those long nails that Jim Carrey has in *Dumb and Dumber*—the ones that need a power saw—not sexy. They also have health risks: if you leave the fungus unchecked, that junk can spread, invade other parts of your body, and even affect performance *up there*. So clip.

Zap your warts. It's not embarrassing to get warts. It happens. It's embarrassing, however, when they go untreated. A quick trip to the doctor's will freeze the fuckers off. There's really no excuse, and nothing will kill the mood of romance better than, "Hey . . . what's this weird wart? Do you have an STD?"

Tame the jungle. As Christina Applegate says to Will Ferrell in *Anchorman*, "You have way too much pubic hair." That might work for Ron Burgundy—he's kind of a big deal—but the twenty-first-century woman prefers tidiness.

Un-stank your feet. You're making out. Scratching. Clawing. Groping. The shirts fly off, she plunges her tongue down your throat, you kick off your shoes . . . and the room fills with the odor of rotted milk and sour eggs. If your feet smell like feet, pay a visit to the good Dr. Scholl.

Trim your nose hair. Three things will make you look older than your age: a premature receding hairline, a wedding ring, and visible strands of nose hair. Compounding matters, the moment a girl sees nose hair, that's the only thing she'll be able to focus on. She can't look you in the eyes or listen to your words—she's now obsessed with the hair of horror. It's the bizarro opposite of you and cleavage.

MAXIM IN ACTION

One more thing: pit stains. I'm a heavy sweater. So this one's a challenge I've grappled with my entire life. Over seventy-six degrees and I'm sweating. But vigilance goes a long way, as you can avoid certain shirts (gray tees, for example) that are prone to moisture. Undershirts help. Trimming pit hair (which just *barely* avoids a violation of MAXIM #49) helps. Like fighting terrorism, we'll never have an absolute victory, but that's no excuse for waving the white flag of surrender.

MAXIM EXCEPTIONS

What if you're happily (or unhappily) married and you have no need to seduce new women? Tough. Frankly, your wife puts up with the other ninety-nine maxims in this book, which, from her (and any logical person's) perspective, are dubious at best, insulting at worst. The least you can do: give her feet that don't stink.

MAXIM #39

TEST YOURSELF.

YOU NEED TO get *those* kinds of tests. You know: those. Bear with me, okay? Yes, this sounds about as fun as "Eat your vegetables" or "Don't play next to the power lines" or "Stay in school, kids."

But it's nonnegotiable. Flings, hookups, and casual sex are all fun and games until someone gets chlamydia. With 15 million new flare-ups of STDs in the United States every year, you have 15 million reasons to get tested. Keep the following in mind:

Some STDs don't have symptoms. You don't need to have a burning sensation, blisters, or a green penis to be infected. Scary? Yes. So the only way to know is to get tested.

The good news: it's cheap. No health insurance is no excuse. Plenty of public clinics will test you for free; just google "free public std test [your city]" and you'll find options. And even if it costs some dough, bite the bullet. If you can afford the date that led to sex, then you can afford to make sure your junk doesn't fall off.

Timing matters. If you have an undiagnosed STD that affects your immune system, this increases your odds of accruing *more* STDs. So nip it in the bud.

It's not like parallel parking. When you're sixteen or seventeen years old, you have the feared parallel parking exam as part of your driver's test, and then you're done for life—no more tests. STDs are a slightly different creature; a clean slate at age 22 doesn't mean squat at 37.

MAXIM IN ACTION

I once dated a girl and it didn't end well. (A first.) A couple of months later—no texts, no e-mails, no calls—at 3 A.M., I get the following text from her:

> Hey. I think I have herpes
> and might have given it to
> you. Just FYI.

I call her back and get voicemail. I call her again and get voicemail. Nothing. So I start to freak out. I make a list of every girl I've been with since her, and I start to think about who *I'd* have to call. I make a doctor's appointment. I spend three hours on WebMD looking at pictures of rotting penises. It was a fun night. The next day she sends another text:

> hey. false alarm. sent that
> text while drunk to every guy
> ive been with in past year.
> heard from doctor. its only
> a UTI.

Huh. Well, thanks for the heads-up. In hindsight, it was a blessing in disguise: it's amazing how a little scare will slap you with the fear of God and take this stuff more seriously.

MAXIM EXCEPTIONS

If you're stuck in a marriage or slogging through a long-term monogamous relationship, then obviously you don't need this test. If you were tested seven years ago and haven't had sex since, well, this is your only good news: you're as clean as you are miserable.

MAXIM #40

PROPERLY ORDER A STEAK.

IT'S NOT NECESSARY to be a steak snob, but you should know the cuts, know how to spot a tenderloin from porterhouse, and know that you should never—*ever*—order your beef well done. Some girls will think you suck in bed. For real. They think you'll suck at doing certain . . . things. As my friend Amy says, "A guy who doesn't like his steak juicy and pink in the middle makes me think he doesn't like *anything* juicy and pink in his mouth."

Along with knowing how to order your steak, you must observe these three additional rules of table etiquette, particularly when on a date:

Figure 4.10.
A rare time to be high-maintenance.

No coupons. Unless you're so comfortable with your date that you can openly belch or pick your nose, it's unacceptable for you to whip out a special for 10 percent off. Granted, this contradicts a more global rule that you care more about substance than style, that you appreciate frugality, that you never flaunt wealth. How to explain this paradox? You're adhering to a rule that's even more transcendent: when it comes to the possibility of sex, you never take it slow (see MAXIM #30). A coupon saves you more than 10 percent . . . it also saves the $1 that you won't be spending on a condom.

Get dessert. It doesn't matter if you're so stuffed, so bloated, that you feel like Al Bundy unbuttoning your jeans so your gut can expand. When you're on a date, you order dessert. It's her role to want it but not say it, it's your role to not want it but say it. Think of it as the opposite of sex.

Know how to pair wines. Don't be that guy who marvels at the floating "legs" or the "bouquet," but you should know enough to avoid embarrassment. When you have utterly no clue on what to select, go

87

for the "third bottle from the bottom" on the price list, and order it with confidence.

MAXIM IN ACTION

Another thing: you can handle spices. If not? Remember, milk products will tame the burn. So don't get buffalo wings without ranch; order sour cream with your Mexican; and if you're eating Indian, get the raita. This ensures that you can finish your meal and save face in front of any friends (or girls) without mockery. Dairy products will not, however, save you from tomorrow's hot butt.

MAXIM EXCEPTIONS

Dinner with the boys? All rules get chucked out the window. Bring in a manila folder stuffed with coupons and leaf through to find the best deal, scrimp on dessert, and pair your steak with the cheapest bottle of house Chianti. You're not worried about impressing your buddy Joe. That being said, you still shouldn't order it well done.

PART V.
STYLE

MAXIM #41

NO MAN MAKEUP.

A WAR RAGES in every man's soul. Two forces clash: the desire to look good and the desire to act like a man. In certain rare cases these two overlap: lifting weights, running marathons, chivalrously buying the girl more alcohol.

Most of the time, however, we find tension—incompatibility, even—between these two dueling impulses. The most hotly contested issue? Grooming. It's a complicated subject with no easy answer.

The Neanderthal camp of "burly manly men" contends you only need to buy two grooming products, ever: toothpaste and a stick of deodorant. If they had it their way, the deodorant could be smeared on teeth, too. In the other camp: metrosexuals, whose shaving kits look like Revlon catalogs.

So this is when I launch into a mock-outraged, puffy-chested dia-tribe against the effeminate pansy metrosexuals, right? Actually, no. It's not that simple. Consider the goal of the metro: He's optimizing his looks so that women will find him more attractive, allowing him to have *more sex with more women.* You have to admit . . . this approach isn't without merit.

Let's follow the metro approach to its only logical conclusion. To *truly* optimize your appearance would require getting "calf implants" like Johnny Drama on *Entourage.* You'd need to get electrolysis to make your body smooth and flawless and hairless. Undergo surgery to inject your lips with collagen. Splurge for regular manicures and pedicures.

At that point, you're tempted to just go for it and start wearing pantyhose and high heels. Why not, right? They make your legs look great. You start using rouge. A little eye shadow. Blush. And soon you'll wonder, heck, why do I still have this silly penis? So you get that little issue taken care of, too.

So we must draw a line. And that line is man makeup.

MAXIM IN ACTION

You're violating this maxim if your bathroom contains any of the following six products:

(1.) **Night cream.** A guy is permitted to apply exactly one type of cream to his face: shaving. (Your shaving cream, however, may be of the expensive variety. It's not a scam: that stuff works.)

(2.) **Anything from Sephora.** If you're asking what "Sephora" is, good, you're in the clear.

(3.) **Skin revitalizers.** Your skin is plenty vital enough, thanks.

(4.) **Eye cream.** I'll be honest. I don't really know what this is, but it sounds suspiciously like eyeliner or eye shadow.

(5.) **Self-tanning lotion.** Not only have you lost your virility, you look like an orange gnome, too (also, see MAXIM #49).

(6.) **Concealer.** The only thing you should conceal is emotion and insecurity (see MAXIMS #1–100).

MAXIM EXCEPTIONS

If you have a punishing case of acne, abandon these guidelines. Treat it. Buy your vials and "complexion solution" and whatever other manners of witchcraft you need. You get a pass. No man should be forced to have a face that looks like a cranberry muffin.

MAXIM #42

SHOP WITHOUT "GOING SHOPPING."

MEN HAVE A complicated relationship with commerce. We appreciate it. We know it has merit. We tip our hat to millennia of economic progress: markets, transactions, supply and demand.

We're not philistines. Gone are the days when we harvest our own crops, hunt our own dinner, stitch our own clothes from the skin of our goats. We get it. We acknowledge that, yes, from time to time, we must pay for goods and services, we must go to a store, we must buy things.

But going to the store is fundamentally, radically different from "going shopping." One is efficient. The other frivolous.

Men especially don't "go shopping" together. It's not an authorized form of male bonding. Take the extreme example. Even if you and your buddy both need to buy a pair of jeans, and if you both happen to be having lunch together (authorized activity) within a block from the jeans store (you don't know any better than to call it a "jeans store"), and if it would actually *save time* to run the errand together, and if there's a two-for-one deal . . . it's still forbidden. Never put yourself in a position where you're staring at your buddy's ass, evaluating whether his butt looks good, contemplating whether his package fits snug against the fabric.

MAXIM IN ACTION

Let's say a man needs to buy a new pair of shoes. Left to his own devices, he would simply buy shoes in bulk, stuffing his closet with fifty identical pairs of sneakers that will last until he dies. Alas, the fickle gods of Fashion would smite him down, so he turns to women for guidance.

At the girl's recommendation he goes to a shoe store, then flips each shoe upside down and looks at the sticker price, seeking the cheapest one that she'll approve. This is not fun. It's not a movie montage of trying on new looks, preening in the mirror to the sounds of "Pretty Woman" or "Material Girl." The entire operation should take seven minutes. If you get home and the shoe doesn't fit, you decide to suck it up and keep 'em, choosing two years of discomfort over an extra second of shopping.

MAXIM EXCEPTIONS

For certain rare purchases, we need proper research to ensure a sound investment. When a guy needs to buy a new Blu-ray player, say, it's prudent to spend several hours in Best Buy, leisurely roaming every aisle of the store, browsing through scanners, digital cameras, TV wall-mounting units (even if we don't have a TV or a wall to mount it on), and 1,000-tetrabite external hard drives. We don't have a tetrabite of data—frankly, we're a little fuzzy on the meaning of "tetrabite"—but damn if it doesn't sound impressive.

This isn't hypocrisy. This is shrewd financial planning. Unlike sweaters or sunglasses, technology interlocks and forms the home's connective tissue, so buying a printer requires a deep, thorough investigation into the newest line of home stereos. The same goes for hardware, cars, and Christmas trees.

MAXIM #43

NO BATHS.

PLUMBING HAS COME a long way since the Romans dumped water in a bucket. As men, we embrace this newfangled technology called a "shower." It's simple. It's effective. It's quick. When you're old enough to clean your body without your mother or a rubber ducky, you are forbidden from taking baths.

Let's start with cleanliness. In this one area, men have a superior grasp of personal hygiene. When you take a bath, you literally wallow in your own filth. As the grime peels from your armpits, it swirls in the water and reenters through your nostrils. It's the fourth law of thermodynamics: the amount of slime in the bathtub cannot increase or decrease, it merely redistributes.

Men get dirty. Imagine a bath after sawing lumber or changing the oil or mowing the lawn. The clear water darkens. It fills with leaves and twigs and clumps of dirt. If a casual onlooker walked in the bathroom, they'd think the man had dunked himself in a septic tank and wonder why he was "cleaning" his face with murky brown water.

"But that's not me," you argue. "I'm not a farmer. I'm not a mechanic at Jiffy Lube." You say that you don't get that dirty; a bath works just fine. You have just a thin veneer of sweat that easily fizzles into the water, making baths a pleasant, relaxing way to end your day.

You are clearly at risk of lighting scented candles, sprinkling exotic salts into the water, injecting your bath with bubbles, painting a green mud mask over your face, sipping a nice Riesling, flipping on some Enya, thinking that when you're finished, maybe you'll have time to shave your legs.

Figure 5.3. *Don't let this happen to you.*

MAXIM IN ACTION

Remember that scene from *Rocky* when Sylvester Stallone took a bath? How about that time Clint Eastwood killed a rapist with a shotgun, crushed a dude's windpipe, and then relaxed with a nice bubble bath? Me neither. This one's almost impossible to see "in action" because it's simply *not done*.

MAXIM EXCEPTIONS

If you travel to a foreign country that has baths and no showers, you may do what you must. Bathe. But don't get carried away: no bubbles or candles or fragrances. Your bath is a necessary evil. Keep it brisk and workmanlike; grumbling about a lack of showers is encouraged and helps retain your gender identity.

The far more critical exception: you may (and should) take a bath with a woman. No maxim would ever deprive you of bath sex. Does this mean you have a free pass? Absolutely not. Your time in the tub may not include actual hygiene or washing your hair, but instead must focus squarely on sex and foreplay (preferably not in that order). And to help restore balance, it's recommended that you offset every session of candled, sensitive, bathtub lovemaking with at least one shower fuck.

MAXIM #44

ONLY WEAR SUNGLASSES WHEN IT'S SUNNY.

YOU WOULDN'T WEAR scuba goggles to a wedding. You wouldn't wear a ski mask to a party. You wouldn't wear shoulder-pads to the movies. You wear accessories when you need them. You value function.

So why would you wear sunglasses indoors—where there's no actual sun? There are only three possible reasons:

Reason 1: You're clinically stupid. You really don't understand that when you're indoors, the lighting is already set to a comfortable level that poses no risk to your cornea. It honestly has never occurred to you that it's darker with your sunglasses on; you chalked it up to a headache or fever. If this is your reason, if you are certifiably, clinically stupid, you go ahead and wear those sunglasses, and you wear 'em with pride, buddy. It's the least you deserve from this cruel, unforgiving world.

Reason 2: You're Homer Simpson lazy. The act of flicking your sunglasses on and off—again and again, throughout the day—is more of a chore than you can stomach. Which makes sense—until you follow this thinking to its logical conclusion. Why button your fly? You just have to unbutton next time you take a leak. Why wear a shirt? You just have to strip next time you take a shower. Why wipe your ass? It's just getting dirty again.

Reason 3: You think it's stylish. This one makes the *least* sense. It's not stylish. It's try-hard. It's cartoonish. It's transparent that you really, really want to look fashionable and trendy, that you'll even *impair your vision* so you can sit with the cool kids in the cafeteria. Still skeptical? Still want to "wear your sunglasses at night"? Consider the song. And if you think Corey Hart is stylish, this book can't solve your larger problems.

MAXIM IN ACTION

Let's think about the indoor-sunglass wearer. This is the same guy who waved a glow stick in the late nineties, and maybe even rocked some of those glow-in-the-dark braces. This is the white guy who still calls his buddies "Dog." He still says, "Why you gotta be a Hater," and when his friends tire of that, he says (like it's his original joke), "Shut up and drink your Haterade!" This is the guy who wears designer tracksuits when he's going nowhere near a track.

MAXIM EXCEPTIONS

- If you're plagued by an ocular disease that makes your eyes ultrasensitive to light, you have a 24/7, weekdays and weekends "anytime minutes" policy with sunglasses. But don't get used to it. When your inflammation passes, so does your waiver.
- If you are George Clooney.
- If you have been beaten up, indoor sunglasses are a sanctioned method for cloaking your black eye. Note: this is permitted but inadvisable, as a black eye is testament to your virility.

MAXIM #45

HAVE THE GUTS TO WEAR PINK.

YOU'VE HEARD "REAL men don't wear pink." Forget it. Shit-can it. That's outdated philosophy, bad intelligence. You live in a new generation with new rules. You can wear pink. In fact, you get *credit* for wearing pink.

Women like it. They appreciate your sense of flair, sense of adventure. It's bold and confident. But the key, as in censorship and salt, is moderation. A pink tie with a black suit is the ideal flourish. A pink tie with a pink suit is the ideal extra for *To Wong Foo*.

Don't be afraid to wear pink. You should, however, be afraid to wear the following:

Tight pants. A good rule of thumb: they're too tight if we can tell whether you dress to the left or to the right.

Jeans shorts. Unless the ragged, frayed material matches the bottom of your mullet.

Sweater tied around your waste. Unless you're a Kennedy and you're on Cape Cod and you somehow traveled back to 1964.

Shirts that show midriff. On a woman, that sliver of skin between her shirt and her jeans is tantalizing and sexy. On a man, it's only moderately less scarring than the plumber's ass crack.

Highlights in your hair. Not only does this violate MAXIM #46 on haircuts, it's a transparent display of vanity.

Banana swimsuit. Maybe someday a male lingerie company will launch a provocative, daring new campaign with the slogan "Bring back the bulge," but thankfully, that day is still decades in the future. Keep your junk hidden.

Figure 5.5.
The enemy.

A beret. Less than 1 percent of the population can pull this off. If you're not sure if you're included in that 1 percent, you're not.

MAXIM IN ACTION

The pink tie–black suit combo is particularly lethal. Think of it as the "Social Power Tie." And wearing it when you are *not* expected to dress up is a surefire conversation starter. When you wear the pink tie and black suit to a bar, say, it's the male equivalent of cleavage. Girls will look at it. They'll even stare at it. Pickup strategies involving "props" (and there are many) deserve suspicion, but the suit is a classic way to wedge (see MAXIM #81).

MAXIM EXCEPTIONS

While you shouldn't be *afraid* to wear pink, by now it should also be clear that you can't be so fashion focused, so obsessed with your image, that you spend more than ninety seconds plotting your outfit. In fact, the word "outfit" gets under your skin and doesn't feel right. It's not. Pink is a handy shortcut. It gives women the illusion that you know something about style, even though, as per MAXIM #2, you can barely recognize the color.

MAXIM #46

SPEND MORE ON BEER
THAN HAIRCUTS.

WE MEN ARE flexible. We're willing to go with the flow. In an ideal world, we'd only get haircuts when our ropey, tangled manes actually impaired our vision or tripped our feet. But we compromise. We get haircuts at least once a month, conforming to accepted (if arbitrary) standards of grooming.

Yet we don't enjoy it. We don't look forward to it. In fact, we usually don't *think* about it until our girlfriend badgers us. And we certainly, absolutely don't *strategize* about it.

There's no maxim against looking good (for a more robust discussion on the matter, see MAXIM #41 on man makeup), but your haircut should be efficient and economical, not a pampered trip to a spa. As a rule of thumb, your haircut may not be more expensive than your weekly budget for beer. If you're an alcoholic—half your budget.

One sign that you have an unseemly, gender-inappropriate problem: Your haircut requires an appointment, as opposed to the time-honored tradition of walking into the barbershop, flipping through a four-month-old *Sports Illustrated*, and watching *Out for Justice* on VHS. (Random tangent: barbershops just might be the only remaining purchasers of VHS tapes; curiously, they're almost always Steven Seagal or early '90s movies. Look for it next time.)

Other symptoms: you have a "stylist" instead of a barber. Your stylist is a woman, and she doesn't just ask you how you want it. She brainstorms. She consults. She wants to experiment. She has a long-term "vision" for your hair that involves texture and color and body.

MAXIM IN ACTION

If you get your hair cut at a place that has "technicians," sells products like "illuminating primer," and offers manicures and pedicures, you're probably in the wrong place. If the guy next to you is covered in a facial mask, you're probably in the wrong place. If candles are burning, you're probably in the wrong place.

MAXIM EXCEPTIONS

You may splurge for a haircut if you're ugly. Please don't take offense. It's not your fault. But a great haircut can be a handicap, of sorts, for guys who were born with a face like Larry Bird. Let's be honest. When girls are born ugly, they can hide it with thousands of remedies like frosted eye shadow, blush, skin gloss, foundation, maple cream, translucent powder, and mascara.

Pop quiz: I made two of those up.
If you know which two, you fail.

Ugly girls have a means of looking better. Guys? We have nothing. Working out can improve your overall appearance, but from the shoulders up, a killer haircut is the only viable option.

MAXIM #47

IGNORE WINDOW TREATMENTS.

IF YOU'RE NOT married or living with your girlfriend, right now you should be asking yourself one very simple question: what in holy hell is a "window treatment"? If you don't know, you're off the hook. This chapter isn't for you . . . yet.

If you've heard of window treatments? You should have one (and only one) reaction to those words: your heart should plummet. "Window treatments" should sound like "detention" to a high schooler or "pick up my soap" to an inmate—it's the scourge of your relationship, two little words that can butcher your Saturday.

In the interest of my own sanity I can't risk proper research, so let's lean on Wikipedia: "In interior decorating, a window treatment may refer to any of the following items placed over or around a window: curtains or drapery, including sheers; window blinds, Venetian blinds, and plantation shutters; a valance; tiebacks used to hold curtains."

It's too painful. I can't even reread that last paragraph. (Plantation shutters?! Make it stop.) What you *do* care about, though, is function. You admit that it's important to cover your windows with *something*. This way you can watch your flat-screen TV (see MAXIM #65) without glare from the sun, dim the lighting for hangovers, and have sex on the floor without giving the UPS dude a free peepshow.

As for the treatments themselves? Why does this deserve its own maxim? Because it's symbolic of a broader philosophy about interior decorating: you have utterly no preference. None. You're happy with miniblinds. Or curtains. Or a dark blanket, or maybe a nice slab of plywood. You just don't give a damn.

Figure 5.7. *You don't know what this is called.*

At the risk of perpetuating gender stereotypes (little joke), life has a certain natural order. She

103

gets drapery and you get the garage. The second you violate this unspoken compact is the second you've ruined it for the rest of us.

MAXIM IN ACTION

The most flagrant violation is when a guy not only cares about curtains but actually *himself* initiates a conversation about window treatments, even invoking that hellish phrase. This not only violates good taste, it jeopardizes your relationship. Sure, girls like guys who are sensitive, but there's sensitive and then there's . . . Venetian blinds. Toe that line. Never cross it.

MAXIM EXCEPTIONS

Functionality matters. There are rare times when to maximize your functionality, you actually really do have to consider the stuff that goes on your windows. While plywood might be effective in blotting out the sun, certain unfortunate, real-world constraints could create complications. (Like, say, your house would look like it belongs to the Unabomber, you couldn't *ever* see sunlight, and your marriage would collapse.)

If you have a specialized need for pitch-darkness—maybe you're a heavy drinker and need to snooze in the afternoon—you may consider your windows. This might require you to browse though many different curtains, weigh the pros and cons of miniblinds, and even— yes—consider the Venetians. But make it quick. Don't enjoy it. And for God's sake, don't use the words "window treatment."

MAXIM #48

DRESS YOUR AGE.

BEWARE THE "SLOB trap." On the one hand, as we've already discussed, you're not obsessed with Marc Jacobs, "going shopping" (MAXIM #42), or the hot new trends on the catwalk. When you flip through your girlfriend's fashion magazine while sitting on the can, your mission is to ogle cleavage, not marvel at the new spring handbags.

That does *not*, however, give you license to dress like Turtle from *Entourage*. It's time to hang up the ironic, large font "I'm not a gynecologist, but I'll take a look!" T-shirt.

It's time to dress your age. The benefits? It shows the world you're aging gracefully, that you're self-confident, and that you're not still trying to pick up high school girls. As an added bonus, high school girls love it.

The sub-maxims:

No saggy jeans. Underwear is called underwear for a reason. Maybe you're all proud of yourself for plunking $60 on Armani boxers, but this is the kind of overcompensation you show a girl in private, not public.

No hipster belts. My buddy Kabir—34, consultant, works with Excel pivot tables—wears a belt that has a giant-sized Superman logo. A good rule of thumb for Kabir (and all of us) to follow: you probably shouldn't wear it on a date if it blends right in at Chucky Cheese.

No Hawaiian shirts. Dressing your age also means that you shouldn't dress like a 78-year-old playing the nickel slots at the Golden Nugget.

No ironic T-shirts. We get it. When you wear a T-shirt that says in big block letters "DORK," what you're really saying is that you're actually *not* a dork, and that you're the baddest motherfucker for having the balls to wear it. It's not cute. It's not clever. And it's played out. Dork.

No leather pants. Unless you're also wearing garish white face paint and you're smack in the middle of Tommy Thayer and Gene Simmons.

No visors at night. In the thousands of bars across the nation, I've yet to find one that's illuminated by a light that's so bright, so searing, that it requires a protective visor.

No trucker hats. Unless you actually drive a truck, in which case you automatically have enough butch points to break the other ninety-nine maxims, too.

MAXIM IN ACTION

The 40-year-old dude who dresses like a frat boy is only a small step from being Creepy Guy in the corner of the dance club, the one who eyes all the incoming girls, sipping his beer, toying with his zippered bag of roofies. This isn't to say that dressing inappropriately will *necessarily* turn you into a sexual predator. But it doesn't help.

MAXIM EXCEPTIONS

Once you've conquered your chosen profession and achieved global fame, at that point, you may dress however you damn well please. How else can we explain Snoop Dogg and his hats, Jerry Seinfeld and his sneakers, Kanye West and his sunglasses (or are they protective goggles?), and Matthew McConaughey, who has made the incredible decision to only appear in public wearing swim trunks?

MAXIM #49

NO FAKE AND BAKES.

FINE. I'LL PUT my cards on the table: I'm pasty white. When bare-chested, it looks like I'm still wearing an ultrafitted white T-shirt. It's impossible for me to tan: instead of getting that golden shade of brown, my skin first turns pink, then red, then blistery and bubbly.

Even if I lounged on the beach all summer, I'd get about as tan as Hurley gets thin on *Lost*. So this maxim hits very, very close to home. If anyone should fake and bake, it's me.

Is it tempting? You bet. The thought of hitting a tanning booth twice a week, taking a nap, and emerging with a Greek-statue torso (minus the whole six-pack thing) . . . yeah, it's intriguing. I daydream. I flip through coupons. I go online and check out prices.

And then I remember . . . I'm not in a sorority. I'm not trying to look hot in a bikini. I'm not trying to impress my ex-boyfriend whom I might see at the ten-year high school reunion. I'm not hoping that I can wiggle into my bridesmaid dress.

True, there's something to be said for wanting to look good. (For a fuller analysis, see MAXIM #41 on man makeup). The governing principle, however, is for men to improve their appearance through a naturalistic approach.

A male fake-and-bake smacks of vanity and frivolity. Related taboos:

No waxing your legs or underarms. It's not just unmanly: it's creepy. You may, however, wax your back and shoulders. In the last 400 years, no woman has ever said, "Your back-hair is really sexy."

No manicures and pedicures. True, some men are so comfortable with their sexuality—so secure in their own skin—that they can pamper their nails like women. And that's a wonderful thing. Hopefully, some day soon, these men will be allowed to get married in more than a couple of states.

No waxed eyebrows. You'll look like a *Sesame Street* puppet. It's not a bad idea, though, to pluck in between. No maxim would ever condemn you to being a uni-brower.

MAXIM IN ACTION

The *40-Year-Old Virgin* demonstrates that the key to bedding Catherine Keener (or any woman, presumably) is not, in fact, a tan and hairless slab of chest. After literally *bleeding* during his chest waxing (this wasn't a special effect; the man actually bled), Steve Carell still had a chest like Chewbacca's white cousin. Only when he abandoned his pursuits of vanity and started "being himself" (ahhhhwwww) did he win the girl's heart. A little schmaltzy? A lot schmaltzy. But sometimes there's truth in syrup.

MAXIM EXCEPTIONS

If you're a cabana boy, actor, or male model—go to hell, by the way—you're permitted to get a fake-and-bake. It's a professional write-off. (Extra credit, though, if you can hack it with your papery-white skin. Not that I'm biased.) If you're a swimmer or contortionist, you may wax your legs and arms. You may wax your eyebrows if you're Leonard Nimoy.

MAXIM #50

SHAVE.

THERE ARE MANY acceptable ways to express yourself: civilized protests, written missives, flipping the bird. But some guys try and get cute. They use facial hair to say something bold, something provocative, something shocking that will put the world on its heels.

This is nothing new. Throughout history, even great men have made unfortunate choices with facial hair. Zeus was the father of all gods but could not, for all his omnipotence, squeeze in time to see a barber. Charles Dickens had a wooly mop that dangled from his nostrils. Perhaps if Trotsky had trimmed his bushy mustache more than once a month, he would have commanded more respect and defeated Stalinism. We'll never know.

MAXIM IN ACTION

So if you're Zeus, or the most prolific novelist in the English language, or a Russian revolutionary, feel free to ignore this maxim. Otherwise you may never grow the following:

Goatee/Fu Manchu Hybrid: You've seen it. It's the goatee that wasn't quite finished, as if the guy just couldn't bring himself to connect the bottom half, sort of like Hulk Hogan's. Here's the thing about Hulk Hogan: he's kinda compelling because he's kinda freaklike. You're only one step removed from wearing yellow tank tops and kissing your guns and snarling, "What'cha gonna do, what'cha gonna do, Brother, when [your name] mania runs wild on you?"

Muttonchops: We get it. By growing your sideburns to levels not seen since the Civil War, you're brandishing your independence and your backbone: why be a slave to convention, you say? Fair enough. Just think about this. What kind of girl do you suppose you'll attract with this tactic—the girl of your dreams or the girl who doesn't shave her legs?

Handlebar mustache: If you're a diabolical villain who wears a stylish top hat (à la Daniel Day Lewis in *Gangs of New York*), go ahead and rock the handlebar. If you're a hipster who thinks it's ironic, go ahead and choke yourself.

ZZ Top Beard: It's a tempting world view: "If it's good enough for Karl Marx, shouldn't it be good enough for me?" Only one problem. His beard works about as well as communism and gets even less ass.

MAXIM EXCEPTIONS

When a guy reaches a certain level of fame and sex appeal, it wouldn't matter if he grew a garden on his chin, bathed himself in horseradish, yellowed his teeth, and gained forty pounds of flab. He could do all this and your wife would *still* ditch your relationship to sleep with him. Go ahead and google "Brad Pitt beard." It's scary stuff. And you know what? He's still sexier than you. And also, for perplexing reasons, Major League relief pitchers—Al Hrabosky, Dustin McGowan—are rife with curious facial hair. Unless you're one of them or Brad Pitt or Zeus, buy a can of Barbasol.

PART VI.
WORK

MAXIM #51

NO EXCLAMATION POINTS OR EMOTICONS!!! :-)

IF A PICTURE'S worth a thousand words, a punctuation mark is worth the sum of a man's character. Is this because we adore grammar? Because we just frickin' love proper syntax? Because we give a damn about split infinitives?

No. This has nothing to do with grammar, and everything to do with not acting like a prepubescent girl. At the workplace—or any place, really—you should rarely press shift while pressing the "1" key. And never do this: :-)

You're skeptical. You're pulling back. You're unwilling to commit to this particular maxim. *Really?* What do exclamation points have to do with me?

The guy who abuses exclamation points is the guy who awkwardly claps coworkers on the back— big hearty backslaps that make everyone uncomfortable—he's the guy who belly-laughs at the boss's bad jokes.

Doesn't this look corny! And overeager! Like you're gunning for a promotion! Allrighty!

omg!

;-)

Figure 6.1. *You are not a teenage girl.*

When you strip your e-mails of exclamation points, you sound less like a dweeb and more like Humphrey Bogart. You sound confident. Sure of your decisions. Whenever you think you *need* an exclamation point to convey the right tone, you're almost invariably wrong.

Let's try it.

"Have a good trip! ;)" becomes **"Have a good trip."**

The first was written by a kid. The second by a man.

"Nice work on the forecast!" becomes **"Nice work on the forecast."**

The first was written by a sycophant. The second by someone who doesn't give praise lightly, whose opinion carries weight.

MAXIM IN ACTION

In my former life as a marketing database analyst, I had a coworker who used an exclamation point with every sentence. He sounded like he was on meth! No one liked the guy! Probably not coincidentally, he did the least work in the group!

One day we felt bad for the guy because he had some genuinely tragic news: his grandfather passed away. We comforted him. We felt for him. He e-mailed the larger group (fifty-plus colleagues) to tell them that he'd be out of the office to attend services.

Guess how he started the e-mail?

"Hi All: My grandpa passed away! I'll be out of the office for the funeral!"

MAXIM EXCEPTIONS

Irony. At times, exclamation points are needed to underscore mocking, skewering, or satire. Let's say you're bantering with a cute coworker, and you're giving her hell for her awful taste in TV. Maybe you IM something like, "Right, I can't *wait* to see the new *Hills*!" If you dropped the exclamation point, she might think you're serious. That would be bad.

The only other exception: An exclamation point can also be used to represent a factorial. 5! would mean $5 \times 4 \times 3 \times 2 \times 1$, or 120. And if you're in a workplace that uses factorials, chances are you're not impressing many women.

MANAGE TIME WITHOUT A TIME MANAGEMENT SYSTEM.

YOU BELIEVE IN getting things done. You don't believe in acronyms, glossy binders, or fancy "time management systems" that waste your time. Same goes for theories on leadership or management. When HR compels you to attend an all-day workshop on the "Fourteen Pillars of Communication," you either play hooky or you play your phone's Brickbreaker.

MAXIM IN ACTION

Since you hate the time management acronyms HR shoves down your throat, you've created one of your own. It describes your thoughts on company pep rallies, leadership summits, time management techniques, safety seminars, seven habits, and the like:

Hopelessly Naive. Even if the theories are true in a vague, textbooky kind of way, rarely do they apply to your job or reduce your workload. The mere slogan "GID" (Get It Done—yes, I actually worked at a *Fortune* 500 Company that used this slogan) doesn't actually get it, or anything, done.

Obvious. The core plank of the "system," more often than not, will be something like: "Do the important thing before the unimportant thing." Hot damn! Now that's a good tip.

Reminder of why you want to quit. Occasionally you love your job. You do. There are real moments of fire and passion. But when the consultant spends three days on the importance of communication, you're tempted to communicate your immediate resignation.

Sometimes useful. You're a man of reason. You'll admit it. In most of these sessions, there's a kernel of truth. But it shouldn't take a forty-hour training week to chew a kernel.

Even duller than they sound. They almost always are. When you get the Outlook request for "IMO: Inventory Management Overview" you prepare for the worst, but then it's so painful, so life-sucking, that you envy the bored old lady in *Airplane* who lit a match and doused herself with kerosene.

Sorta Social. You'll give it this much—at least you get to see people outside your usual workgroup. The good news: it's a change of pace. The bad news: the pace is glacial.

Hysterical. One silver lining: usually there's something comically stupid in a Michael Scott or Bill Lombard kind of way.

Insulting. We get it. We don't need to be told that: "To calculate annual profit, deduct the firm's expenses from the revenue." No shit. Everyone knows that. Except for dot-coms, the housing market, and Congress.

Tedious. It's the same thing over and over. The theory will have one basic idea, one format, and then repeat it 100 times, regurgitating the same structure like "Maxim in Action" and "Maxim Exceptions" and—oh. Never mind. You love it when this happens. Repetition is the best.

MAXIM EXCEPTIONS

Plenty of business theories are smart. Some are even useful. You can't deny that Covey's "important vs. urgent" matrix explains a huge swath of office reality; I've drawn the two-by-two grid countless times to break down projects. And sure, books like *Blink, The Tipping Point,* and *The Wisdom of Crowds* have a certain geeky charm. So you're not inflexibly anti-theory. What you are, however, is anti-horseshit. And there's an awful lot of it.

MAXIM #53

UNDERDRINK THE BOSS.

THIS IS NOT some After School Special message that "thou shalt not drink." Far from it. At the dreaded workplace mixer, alcohol acts as a magical pixie dust that makes your coworkers seem like friends, your boss seem tolerable, and even the girls in accounting seem cute.

It's remarkable, really, how just a whiff of booze will improve morale. It even changes how you greet your coworkers. Let's say you work with Derreck all day. When you say good morning, you say "hey" or just shoot him a nod. That's it. For the office party, though—even if you saw Derreck ninety minutes ago when you left work—you'll see him in a bar and bellow, "Heeeeyyyy, D-Money!" and you'll both do the awkward bro-hug (see MAXIM #76). Such is the power of alcohol.

So drink up. However, abide by the following two rules:

Rule #1: Never get drunker than your boss.

This really is part of a larger, more expansive rule: you shouldn't get *noticed* for being drunk. Peer pressure is a helpful benchmark. If everyone is shooting tequila? Grab the limes and salt. If the crowd is nursing a plastic glass of red wine? Rehearse your excuses and plot your escape.

Figure 6.3.
Personal issues.

(Quick tangent: the best excuse to ditch a workplace function? Just tell them that you have to take care of some "personal issues." Do not elaborate. Do not make an apology. When people hear "personal issue," they assume the worst and figure it's so embarrassing, so intimate—like a DNA test to see if you're the father—that they'll drop the question and wish you luck—never realizing that your "personal issue" is to plunk your ass on the couch and play *Grand Theft Auto*.)

Rule #2: No (public) hooking up with coworkers.

It could happen. It will happen. At some point you'll end up sucking face with Allison from marketing. Just wait until you've left (separately, preferably) or at least until you find a secure supply closet.

MAXIM IN ACTION

On my second week on the job, I got plastered with my boss, his boss, and his boss's boss. They drank responsibly and left the bar at midnight. I drank irresponsibly and left the bar at dawn. A few hours later, hung over at my cube, I felt queasy and decided to make my way to the toilet for a nice little barf.

Only one little problem. As I walked to the bathroom, the vomit swelled in my chest and rose faster and faster, erupting up my neck like Mt. Vesuvius. I covered my mouth and walked faster. Still the bathroom was 100 feet away. The vomit gushed. Seventy feet away. The vomit filled my mouth. Fifty feet away. I used both hands to seal my lips, trying to create a dam. Thirty feet away . . . the dam broke. Chunks exploded through my fingers, forming a mushroom cloud of bile that landed . . . right next to my boss, who saw the whole thing.

MAXIM EXCEPTIONS

And the other extreme . . . One hot summer month, to clear my head and focus on writing a screenplay, I gave up booze and sex. Cold turkey. I called it "July is dry." The morning after our Fourth of July office party, the president of our company called me into his office. "Wilser," he said, his voice dead with disapproval. Uh oh. "What's the matter? I understand you weren't drinking last night." Him asking this question might or might not be legal, but clearly I risked losing some cube-cred. Fortunately, I had the presence of mind to tell him I had some personal issues.

MAXIM #54

UR EMAIL CANT LOOKLIKETHIS.

WRITING BAD E-MAILS is like wearing no deodorant. You stink but no one will tell you. And you can't escape it. Like your odor, e-mail is everywhere and affects everyone. It's the lifeblood of your career.

Let's imagine a real-life scenario:

Corporate God takes the escalator down from Corporate Heaven and says in a deep, booming voice:

> *You have broken a maxim. As punishment, I'm taking away one of your abilities. You choose which one.*
> *Option A: You can no longer speak on the phone.*
> *Option B: You can no longer perform real labor.*
> *Option C: You can no longer e-mail.*
> *Your choice?*

No way you give up e-mail. It's more important than virtually any other workplace function. And if you had the guts to ask Corporate God, he'd show you a Holy Excel Book that tabulated this shocking statistic: you've spent more hours e-mailing than you have doing anything else in your waking life. Think about *that.*

Still, whether it's laziness or stupidity, millions of men send millions of e-mails that hav spelling lik tits. We've already covered exclamation points and emoticons (in MAXIM #51! (-:), but the problem is rampant enough, acute enough, that it demands six additional guidelines:

(1.) Avoid gratuitous profanity.

(2.) Keep the fucker brief.

(3.) Assume that *anything* you send from your corporate e-mail account can, and will, be seen by anyone and everyone. No fantasies about how you want to "put a spike in the graph" of Tiffany from accounting. And that really is a fantasy. No one named Tiffany has ever worked in accounting.

(4.) Careful with the Reply Alls. Especially when you're being nasty. Even if they deserved it, calling out someone in a public e-mail chain looks petty, spiteful, and bitchy.

(5.) EASY ON THE CAPS. THEY MAKE THE READER GO BLIND. AND YOU LOOK LIKE A SEVEN-YEAR-OLD.

(6.) Don't have an obnoxious signature or font. If you're the "Managing Director," your subordinate's respect will be earned on the merits of your performance, not because you say **Managing Director** in 14-point Comic Sans.

MAXIM IN ACTION

One more thing: watch your tone. What you intend as a light-hearted attempt at humor might, in the cold medium of e-mail, get misinterpreted as an insult. Like if you said: "Thanks for your 'help' fixing the database. What happened? You really fucked me. You nailed my ass against the wall and pounded, hard, without using a condom or even giving me a reach-around. Just kidding lol."

MAXIM EXCEPTIONS

Not all jobs require heavy e-mail. If you're a goat-herder, perhaps you only need to send a few e-mails a day, and you can do it from your BlackBerry. More importantly, no one's saying your e-mails need to be Shakespeare. Let's not get carried away. Just remember to reread them, spell check, ensure you're not sending porn to your boss, and slap on that digital deodorant.

NEVER VOLUNTEER TO TAKE NOTES.

YOU KNOW WHO he is. He sits at the conference table with his head hunched forward, eager, nodding at the boss. It's not that he's an overachiever, per se; there's nothing wrong with achievements. He's something different. He's an overappeaser.

At some point, this overappeaser will invariably ask with a hopeful lilt in his voice, "Should we be taking minutes?" (Translation for the less-corporate workplaces: "Should we be taking notes?") The room groans. Everyone eye-rolls. Even the boss is slightly embarrassed by this crass, naked opportunism.

Yes, by pulling this little maneuver, you win a few brownie points from your boss. You're seen as a "guy who *gets it*" by the director of marketing. You might get a raise, snare a promotion, score a $10 coupon to Chili's. Kudos.

But you will lose three things.

You will lose self-respect. Do you *really* want to be the guy who fires off Sunday-morning e-mails for no reason, just to make your coworkers look bad? The guy who schedules meetings at 4:30 P.M. on Friday? It will soon sink in that you've slithered up the corporate ladder by stepping on your coworkers' fingers.

You will lose friends. In terms of peer respect, the minute-asker ranks right behind micromanaging bosses and just above sexual harassers.

You will lose any chance of intra-office sex. It might score points with the boys upstairs, but women find requesting minutes about as sexy as having the clap. Which the overappeaser probably has.

Overappeasers aren't made in a day. They start by tattling on their siblings to the babysitter, eager to goose their allowance. They become hall monitors. They hone their skills by asking the teacher— just before the bell rings—if there's any homework for the night. In college, they ratted out their dorm-mates for smoking weed. They tell the president, "Yessir, we'll find 'em, you bet there's WMDs."

MAXIM IN ACTION

Dwight from *The Office*. The classic overappeaser, Dwight would then chronicle the meeting's dialogue with glee, recording every statement, joke, or gesture: "3:47 P.M.: When he thought no one was looking, Jim stuck a finger—index—into his nose to extract mucus." Use Dwight as your role model at your own risk.

MAXIM EXCEPTIONS

Sometimes you actually need minutes. They have their uses. But here's how to handle it: If you feel that someone should take notes, start taking notes. Don't announce it. Don't brag about it. Don't trumpet your anal-retentiveness to the room. And when you've finished, don't make a big show out of e-mailing everyone with "Action Required" items and "Next Steps." There's a fine line between being organized and being a prick.

MAXIM #56

KICK UP, KISS DOWN.

THE SUITS HAVE a saying: Kick up, kiss down. Contrary to what I might have said elsewhere, it's actually okay to kiss a little ass. There's only one catch—you may never kiss the ass of anyone *above* you on the company org chart. Your subordinates, however, you treat like gold.

Put differently, you should always treat your juniors with as much respect—if not more—than your seniors. As a boss, your role is to "kick up" at management (as in kicking ass), sheltering your team from incoming fire.

The reasons are fivefold:

Figure 6.6. *Kick up, kiss down.*

(1.) **You're not a weasel.** Bosses who stomp on their employees and suck up to the executives lack just two things: a left nut and a right nut.

(2.) **That shit's contagious.** Incompetence breeds incompetence, and a mentality of kissing the manager's ass will ooze down to your team, poison morale, and spawn both apathy and backstabbing. For an example of organizations infested with this disease, just go online and type any valid URL that ends in ".gov."

(3.) **Respect.** People believe in a kicker-upper. They'll bleed for him. If their boss says they need to work all weekend, they'll grumble, but they'll work all weekend. Because they know it's for something real, something that matters, like revising the Third-Quarter Budget Forecast that will be revised again next weekend.

(4.) **You don't steal credit.** A corollary to this maxim is that when your employee dreams up some killer idea—selling gasoline online, say—you give him or her credit. Build them up. Encourage them. Besides, the buck stops with you, so ultimately, you'll get the credit. . . whether you like it or not.

(5.) **Your unflagging respect for merit.** If ass-kissery is expected by your boss, fuck him, you didn't want to work there, anyway. Someday you'll quit. Just like you said three years ago and two years ago, this year, you'll quit.

MAXIM IN ACTION

When my sister was selling Girl Scout cookies, my stepdad refused to bring the order form into the office. This drove her mad. Pleading, she argued that they'd buy oodles of cookies (since he was their boss), thus making her the ultimate sales champion. But he held his ground. He said that was precisely the point: since he was their boss, his employees would feel *compelled* to buy twenty boxes of Thin Mints and Caramel deLites, putting them in an unfair position. So he stood up to his 8-year-old daughter (no easy task) and sheltered his employees—kissing down.

MAXIM EXCEPTIONS

This isn't to say that you *must* treat your employees with kid gloves. Obviously there's a time and place for being the bad guy. The place is at work. The time is after you've clearly communicated standards, and they've clearly failed to uphold them. This is how well-run governments operate; when the heads of a financial institution clearly fail, for example, we punish them by forking over a $700 billion bailout package.

MAXIM #57

NO FACE TIME.

DON'T GET ME wrong. Now and then, we've all had to hold our nose and do a little face time—it's an occupational hazard. Your strategy for getting ahead, however, may not rest on this soggy foundation.

If your company hours are nine to six, say, you're forbidden from being that guy who screws around on Facebook (see MAXIM #79) all day, then loiters until 8 P.M. just to make his coworkers look bad. When you get a promotion, you do it on merit and grit, not perception and flattery.

And here's the beauty of it: when you play it right, the adherence to humane, normal work hours actually makes you look *more* competent. It shows that you're organized, you're efficient, and that you have a backbone. Embrace this attitude: "If you're working four hours longer than your expected workday, then you're doing your job *wrong*."

Or if "merit" isn't your thing, here are three tactics that don't involve face time but make you seem like a star:

(1.) **Proactively issue status updates.** Bosses love this shit. They eat it up. Each week, simply give her a rundown of your current tasks and projects. It doesn't matter if you've done *nothing*. A simple list with phrases like "substantially complete" or "in progress" or "60 percent of objective" will make her think you're on top of your game, and it saves *her* the trouble of contemplating what it is you do all day.

(2.) **Use the phrase "hard stop."** When you're in a meeting in the late afternoon, just before it starts, tell the room you have a "hard stop" at 4:45. You'll be amazed at how that goes over. It sounds official. It sounds like you've got important business that commands your attention, far more important than this circle-jerk of a meeting. They don't have to know that your "hard stop" is simply two-for-one happy hour with your buddy Keith.

(3.) **Set and lower expectations.** If you're expecting a steak dinner and you only get a hamburger, you chew your burger in disappointment. If you're expecting a tofu salad and you get a hamburger, you're wildly delighted. Promise tofu, not the steak.

MAXIM IN ACTION

I had a finance job where I worked three hours a day. Literally. I got to work at 9 A.M., devoured every story on ESPN, kept refreshing the page to see more news, took a ninety-minute break to go to the gym, sliced and diced some pivot tables for a bit, then, if it was warm and sunny, took a nap on the lawn of San Francisco's Embarcadero Center. I left before five. And I hid none of this. I always checked in with my boss, always overdelivered, and every year they were somehow foolish enough to promote me. I felt guilty at first. Shouldn't I be staying late? Then I realized—bosses don't like good desk sitters, they like good(ish) work.

MAXIM EXCEPTIONS

The occasional weekend e-mail? The sporadic late-nighter? Nothing wrong with that. And while you should avoid face time for the sake of face time, you should also avoid giving the impression that you don't give a shit, that you're just a nine-to-fiver punching in, punching out. Just remember . . . you have a hard stop.

MAXIM #58

NO JOKES INVOLVING MASTURBATION.

LET'S SAY YOU'RE giving a speech. Maybe it's the Quarterly Budget Presentation. It's a dry subject, so you want to throw your audience a bone, a little humor, a little something to relieve the tension and reward their patience.

Well I've got some news for you, my friend. In our new touchy-feely workplace, some people—especially women—might be offended when you pause, ad-lib a joke, and then throw down a punch line that involves anal sex, blowjobs, donkey-fucking, dead babies, cripple-porn, or even gang rapes. Back in the day, that's all safe stuff. Now? You're "crossing a line."

Figure 6.8.
No toilet humor.

So you've adapted. You've modified what Internet sites you look at, the acronym "NSFW" has entered your vocabulary, and you're very, very careful about which e-mails you can forward (see MAXIM #54), and to whom, sometimes studying the "To:" field for as long as thirty seconds before verifying that no, you are not accidentally copying your boss on an e-mail link to "2 Girls, 1 Cup."

MAXIM IN ACTION

You also have a sense of what's appropriate—and what's not—when it comes to discussing personal relationships. Small talk is fine. Chatting about the day-to-day of boyfriends and girlfriends is fine. One of these two scenarios is appropriate, and one is not. You should know which is which.

Scenario 1: *Asking a coworker if he had a nice time on his date.* You ask PG-rated questions like: "How was the food? Was the conversation any good? Did you guys connect?"

Scenario 2: *Asking a coworker if he had some nice sex on his date.* You ask R-rated questions like: "How was her rack? Did she have that kinda vibe like, I'm not very hot, so I'm gonna fuck extra hard, extra nasty to make up for it?"

You're allowed to have friends at work. But keep the sex talk where it belongs: Instant Messenger.

MAXIM EXCEPTIONS

The rules depend on the culture of your workplace. I started my career at buttoned-up corporations like Intel. I minded my Ps and even Qs. At a later job, at a smaller company, one girl called another girl "Boobs" (she'd had some work done) and whenever she passed Boobs in the hallway, she'd playfully slap Boobs on the ass. No one seemed to mind. At the holiday party, drunk, the two girls danced and made out. No one seemed to mind. Does this mean that at your laid-back office, you can call a girl Boobs? No. Not only will it get you canned, it's actually, well, um . . . wrong. Women shouldn't feel uncomfortable at work. Neither should men. How'd you like it if women constantly made sexual remarks about *you* and were always feeling you up and grabbing your crotch? Never mind.

MAXIM #59

NO BUZZWORDS.

TWO REASONS TO speak in buzzwords: insecurity or laziness. When you speak, you like to use real words that have real meanings, not a verbal diarrhea of corporate gobbledygook.

For whatever reason, millions of cube folk have made the astonishing decision that in order to be taken seriously, they must speak in a tangled, perverted dialect of the English language. Jargon you should avoid:

- "Win-Win." Something losers say, hoping repetition will turn bullshit into diamonds.
- "Thinking outside the box." Anyone who actually says "thinking outside the box" is very much trapped inside one. This box of theirs is a time machine. It creates the illusion that it's still 1995 and this is still a hot new piece of jargon.
- "Net-Net." It's repetitive and redundant. Technically it means: After everything has been taken into consideration, this is the net result—and this is the net result of that. The net result doesn't need an extra net. That's like saying "Final-Final" or "Pregnant-Pregnant." You're either pregnant or you're not.
- "Give it 110 percent." It's simple, really. If you gave 110 percent, by definition, you'd be dead.
- "Goal-oriented." This is a waste of words. Goal-oriented as opposed to what, butterscotch-oriented? Spiritually oriented?
- "Push the envelope." This phrase was popularized (and, arguably, originated) by Chuck Yeager in Tom Wolfe's *The Right Stuff.* Chuck Yeager pushed the envelope to crack the sound barrier; trimming the costs of your travel budget by 2.6 percent does not constitute "pushing the envelope."
- "Synergy." Frequent use of this word has synergy with never getting laid.

MAXIM IN ACTION

What the boss says: "We're really going to push the envelope with this new goal-oriented inventory system. There's some good synergy with the marketing department, so net-net, at the end of the day, if we give it 110 percent it'll be a win-win."

What the boss means: "Uh, there's a new program for tracking inventory. I don't know how it works. Maybe the guys in marketing know how it works? Can you figure it out? Figure out how to use this or when I talk to the director, I'll blame this shit on you."

MAXIM EXCEPTIONS

As with many exceptions, your loophole is irony. It's perfectly acceptable—encouraged, even—to undercut corporate baloney by using the buzzwords sarcastically. If your boss asks if you're giving him attitude, you can say you're giving him 110 percent.

MAXIM #60

DO THE OPPOSITE.

REMEMBER WHEN GEORGE Costanza decides to do the "opposite" of his normal inclinations? He gets the girl's number, he chews out Steinbrenner, and he's immediately offered a job with the Yankees.

Sadly, the "Opposite George" was contained to one episode, never to be repeated. Until now. To determine the proper way to act at work, just look at what Costanza did, and do the opposite. (If you don't like *Seinfeld*, you should probably skip to the next maxim. And then go fix yourself.)

MAXIM IN ACTION

George: Has sex with the cleaning lady on his desk.

You: There's nothing categorically wrong with sex on the desk or sex with the cleaning lady, but the two combined are generally frowned upon. So keep a healthy distance between yourself and the cleaning lady—and all ladies, really—at your job, given the landmine-strewn environment that is sexual harassment. You're so concerned about being appropriate, in fact, that you refuse to compliment women at work. If she changes her hair from blonde to black, you're paranoid that saying "Nice hair" will get you slapped with a lawsuit, so you ignore it and therefore her. You're always 100 percent appropriate. You're so appropriate it's almost hostile. Except for the holiday party where the two of you get drunk and fuck in the supply closet.

George: Gets revenge by slipping his boss a mickey.

You: While you (generally) don't pursue criminal revenge against your manager, you're convinced that you—always—know more than your boss. He just doesn't get it. He doesn't get the challenges of your job, the absurdity of the red tape, or how the whole operation should be changed. You'll show him. When you get promoted to your boss's job—thus giving you the chance to improve the system—you realize

131

that you had it wrong, it was your new boss's fault, and someday when you get *his* job, you'll change the system.

George: Takes excessive doughnuts from the pastry cart.

You: You're actually okay with this. At least George isn't some namby-pamby who will only eat organic low-fat yogurt. When the pastry cart rolls by, you eat a pastry.

George: Sleeps under his desk.

You: As discussed in MAXIM #57, you avoid "face time." You're in the office for only two reasons: in ascending order of importance, (1) work, (2) avoiding your family.

George: Uses the handicapped bathroom as his own "throne."

You: Ideally you'd like to do your "business" at home, especially if it's a new unisex bathroom where your violent, offensive eruptions can be heard by women. So whenever you're expecting turbulence, you'll wander to another department on another floor—Internal Audit, usually—to drop a deuce.

George: Brings in a calzone for Steinbrenner.

You: You'll bring lunch for your subordinates, but never your superiors. See MAXIM #56 on kicking up, kissing down.

George: Stares at cleavage during a pitch meeting

You: Like Jerry, you keep your cleavage staring to a "peek," and you've mastered the art of looking respectful, courteous, and professional while you ogle her legs.

MAXIM EXCEPTIONS

If you're in a temporary job that's not part of your long-term career, and if your boss is lame and the coworkers are lame and the work is lame, then George is your benchmark. Follow his lead. The only catch . . . it's funny how these "temporary" jobs stretch from weeks to months, then to years, then creep into your thirties, then forties, and before you know it you're traded to another company for a box of chicken.

PART VII.
ENTERTAINMENT

MAXIM #61

DANCE ONLY UNDER DURESS.

HERE'S ONE THING you will never witness. You will never see a group of guys sitting around, drinking beer, planning their night's adventure when one of them suddenly says, with a devilish gleam in his eye, "I know. Let's go *dancing*."

Men don't go dancing. On the list of fun physical activities, it ranks just above running in place and just below scooping up dog shit. Dancing isn't fun. Flailing your arms, jutting your hips, and spastically bobbing side to side is for developmentally challenged children, not grown men.

"Hold on. I see guys at the dance club all the time," you say. True. They make an appearance. And when they're at these clubs . . . they may even dance. But there's a distinction. "Going dancing" at a club is categorically different from dancing when you're at a club. The former implies the intent to dance. The latter implies the intent to have sex.

Figure 7.1. *Saturday nights in hell.*

Dancing is a necessary evil. Guys will suffer the indignity if there's a plausible chance of ass. Think of dancing like sales tax at the liquor store: you don't want to pay it, but you must if you want booze. You'd never actively *look forward* to paying sales tax, but you fork over the 7 percent to buy your bottle of Jack. Dancing is the 7 percent.

It's (mostly) not that we're afraid of looking bad on the dance floor . . . it's that we're lazy. We know that dancing flouts a core principle of physics: bodies at rest tend to stay at rest. If you're at the bar with a beer, you only have three reasons to abandon your post: (1) go home; (2) go take a leak (see MAXIM #5); (3) go talk to a girl. If dancing will help you achieve #3, fine, but it's not an end in and of itself.

As a corollary that demands its own maxim (see MAXIM #69), you have no interest in watching *Dancing with the Stars*. Et tu, Jerry Rice?

MAXIM IN ACTION

Driven partly by *Swingers* and Big Bad Voodoo Daddy, the late '90s ushered in a regrettable, mostly forgettable mini-era of swing dancing. Guys took lessons and bought khakis. In each and every case, however, the guy was either appeasing his woman or looking for one. They weren't seeking the elegant, swooshing joy of twirling through the air.

MAXIM EXCEPTIONS

There are times when you must dance. Weddings. Black-tie galas. Bar mitzvahs. At moments like these, you have to pretend that you actually *enjoy* dancing, and you can't confess—to anyone—that you're miserable. The upside? This buys enough goodwill for you to be a grouchy, nondancing sourpuss for the other 364 days of the year.

YOUR FAVORITE BOOK MAY NOT BE *THE DA VINCI CODE.*

AND IT CAN'T be written by Stephen King. Or Tom Clancy. Or Robert Ludlam. Real men read real books.

You know how in the other maxims you don't care about the fluffy, superficial stuff like labels or pleasantries? There's a flip side to this coin. You *do* care about the junk that matters. Books are junk that matters.

MAXIM IN ACTION

So what are acceptable favorite books? Not even I have the arrogance to tell you. And any "list" is laughably inadequate, courts controversy, and omits choices that are clearly superior. Lists are dumb. So here's a list of virile, masculinity-themed books that weren't assigned in high school—so no gimmes like *The Great Gatsby* or *Hamlet*—but books that every man should read before he dies. If the list strikes you as a little obvious, good, you pass.

Lolita, Vladimir Nabokov
Porn disguised as literature. What's not to like?

The Republic, Plato
Ralph Waldo Emerson once said, "Plato is philosophy and philosophy is Plato." Um, maybe that's a little overkill, but the point is fair enough. If you only read one book of philosophy in your life, this is it.

The Art of War, Sun Tzu
Just don't quote it. That's a move for "That Guy" (see MAXIM #67).

Invisible Man, Ralph Ellison
We've all worked in a boiler room of some sort or another, and we've all had the equivalent of shock therapy.

Collected Short Stories, Ernest Hemingway
For some baffling reason our public schools assign his novels, not short stories. Shame.

Revolutionary Road, Richard Yates
Non even DiCaprio can ruin this bleak, unflinching study of how suburbia, marriage, and compromise can shape the modern man. Best enjoyed with a bottle of whiskey.

Don Quixote, Cervantes
Okay, so this might have been assigned in high school, but chances are it was just an excerpt, and chances are you hated it. Give it another go. If Don Quixote doesn't count as a real man, God knows who does.

Moby Dick, Herman Melville
I'm serious. It's worth the slog. Think of it as your Mt. Everest of reading. If nothing else, bring it to the coffee shop to impress women. Maybe you'll find yourself accidentally liking it.

A Good Man Is Hard to Find (collection of short stories), Flannery O'Connor
Understanding the failings, insecurities, and darkness of mankind is not, obviously, only the province of men.

MAXIM EXCEPTIONS

If you are a member of Dan Brown's nuclear family, you may cherish *The Da Vinci Code* as your favorite book. Don't get me wrong. The man's got a nose for repackaging old ideas with a new, appealing twist. (Not that there's anything wrong with that. Ahem.) If you think it represents great fiction, however, you need to read more fiction.

MAXIM #63

KNOW HOW TO CHUG A BEER.
KNOW NOT TO.

YOU MUST BE able to chug a beer—without setting down the glass, without gasping for breath, and without splattering liquid all over your chest.

This doesn't mean you make it a habit. In fact, just as important as knowing *how* to chug is knowing *when* to chug: almost never. Think of it like nuclear weapons. It's crucial that the United States has them, but it's even more imperative that they're never used.

The same goes for drinking a shot. You must know how to slam a shot and do it without blanching. Like Marion from *Raiders of the Lost Ark*, you can knock back your glass, keep a straight face, and hold steady eye contact as if you didn't just swallow Drano.

Figure 7.3. *Friend.*

Speaking of shots. It must be whiskey, tequila, or vodka. *Maybe*—this depends on your company—you can slip a Jager past the goalie. You may order a Buttery Nipple, Sex on the Beach, Silk Panties, or Redheaded Slut if you're in Amsterdam or the Mustang Ranch in Nevada.

A sensible person might ask the simple question . . . "Why? Girl shots taste like Kool-Aid, and guy shots taste like kerosene. Can't we drink Kool-Aid?"

Because if the bar sold kerosene, you'd drink that, too. In fact, they do: it's called absinthe. And you like it. Liquor is like cold medicine—it's only effective when intolerable.

Your body needs this semiregular test of virility. It's healthy. If your innards can withstand the punishment of 180-proof liquor coursing through your blood, it means you're in peak condition. You're strong. Hardy. Just like Nicolas Cage in *Leaving Las Vegas*.

Do engineers test the safety of cars by racing them at ten miles an hour? Does Kevlar test its vests by poking them with popsicles? Do parachute makers test their chutes by dropping them from the second story? No. They find the limits. You can't test virility with sugar. You must test it with poison. (Disclaimer: I am not a doctor, and if I were, my patients would be dead.)

MAXIM IN ACTION

Three words: Frank. The. Tank. Actually, though, Frank sort of misses the point. It's not that you need to act like a horndog alcoholic, "going streaking" in the quad and sucking down beer funnels. Gross, right? It's that you need to be able to handle your beer like a man. Chugging is your proof, your merit badge.

MAXIM EXCEPTIONS

There's really no reason for you to not at least *once* chug a beer. Again, you don't want to be That Guy who's 30 years old and still crushing beer cans against his forehead. Alternatively, if you abstain from alcohol for religious or personal or medical reasons, no one expects you to chug a beer. (Think about it, though.)

MAXIM #64

YOUR CONTACTS ARE IRRITATED; THOSE AREN'T TEARS.

CONVENTIONAL WISDOM SAYS that even real men, "manly men," are allowed to cry when watching the *Shawshank Redemption, Brian's Song,* or when the fat hobbit picks up the skinny hobbit and carries him up Mount Doom.

This is wrong.

You never cry. Ever. You didn't cry when (spoiler alert) Lassie died. You didn't cry when Buzz reunited with Woody. When ET phoned home, you rolled your eyes and told him, next time, to just send a damn text.

It doesn't mean you didn't like the movies. Morgan Freeman teaching wise, fatherly advice to Tim Robbins while folding laundry—what's not to like? And the secret truth is that yeah, sure, these movies—okay, even *ET*—make you *feel* something. You're not a robot; you just dance like one (see MAXIM #61).

What separates men from women and toddlers, however, is the ability to keep our inside feelings where they belong—the inside. Kleenex tissues may only be used for two bodily fluids: one's mucus and the other isn't tears.

In lieu of crying, you express your emotions by the following outlets:

- Excessive cheering for grown men you've never met, will never meet, and will despise as soon as they start wearing a different color jersey.
- Road rage. If it's supposed to take you thirteen minutes to get to the grocery store and then, because of some ass-clown who cut you off, it takes you thirteen minutes and seven seconds, you will explode in holy rage and uncork your bottled-up feelings.

- Drunken man-love. Although you spend three years hemming and hawing before striking a girl with the L-Bomb (see MAXIM #21), when inebriated, you have no problem telling your bros you love them.
- Geek-outs. Maybe it's *The Watchmen*, maybe it's Bruce Lee, maybe it's Voltron. Whatever it is, it makes your inner geek erupt in joy. She'll never understand so you never tell.

MAXIM IN ACTION

My stepfather has the world's best poker face. He could win the lottery or rupture his spleen—his expression won't change. When he watches movies he stares at the screen impassively, not laughing, not speaking, barely blinking, and sure as hell not crying. When the movie's over? He won't say a word, and we assume he despises it. Then, months later, something curious happens. The movie pops up in his DVD collection. And he watches it over and over, each time with the same impenetrable stoicism. On the fourteenth viewing, it's obvious that he cherishes the movie (Note: never actually use the word "cherish") and that it moved him deeply.

MAXIM EXCEPTIONS

You may cry tears of laughter at movies like *Airplane!*, *Old School*, *Naked Gun*, *Anchorman*, *Dumb and Dumber*, and the like. In some of these movies, you will laugh so hard and weep so openly, that your girlfriend will actually wonder if you are choking or simply retarded. She won't get it. When watching *Dumb and Dumber*, she'll ask if Jeff Daniels drinking a beer bottle filled with urine is really that funny. Which makes you laugh even harder.

MAXIM #65

CONTROL THE WORLD
WITH TECHNOLOGY.

"Whoever controls technology controls the world. The Roman Empire
ruled the world because they built roads. The British Empire ruled the
world because they built ships. America, the atom bomb. And so on and
so forth. I just want what Prometheus wanted."
—Lex Luthor, *Superman Returns*

EVEN IF YOU'RE not creating an artificial island built of Kryptonite,
you understand the value of technology. You like gadgets. You can
rewire speakers. You can set up WiFi.

The Geek Squad is for girls and grandparents. You refuse help
from all outsiders. You spend nine hours crouched behind your TV,
squinting at wires, cursing, wondering why in holy hell Input 1 con-
nects to Output 2. You think about choking yourself with the "audio
digital optical" cable, outraged that it won't synch up with HDMI.
And you love it.

You covet the newest iPhone or BlackBerry, knowing *this* version will make your life complete. You
look at your girlfriend like she's lost her mind when
she asks, confused, whether you *really* need a gizmo
that streams MP3s from your bedroom stereo to your
living room TV. Of course you need it. You need it
yesterday. It's a miracle you got this far without it.

Technology provides focus—vision—to your
home-improvement philosophy. Dropping a hundred bucks on new curtains is like flushing twenties

Figure 7.5. *Today's
perfection, tomorrow's
disappointment.*

down the toilet, but you'll wisely invest $500 (and twenty-plus hours
of installation) on an automated storage-closet lighting system, saving
0.4 seconds every time you would have flipped on the light. And since

you enter that storage closet at least twice a month, those 0.4 seconds really add up.

When you buy a digital camera, it has enough megapixels . . . for now. Roughly eighteen months later, however, the number of megapixels will become frustratingly, tragically insufficient. At that point, a new camera isn't just on your wish list; it's imperative.

MAXIM IN ACTION

Nowhere is your technology religion more important than the advent of flat screens. You can barely remember a world without high-def. Watching a baseball game in standard definition—with the black bars on the sides—is now unthinkable. If your picture isn't sharp enough to count Joba Chamberlain's nose hairs, you might as well be listening to the game on the radio.

Flat screens demand some other changes, too. A brilliant television screen is worthless without content, so you've plotted a move for a Blu-ray player, PS3, and HD-DVR. It would be embarrassing to have gorgeous video with tinny, little-girl speakers, so you've gutted your old stereo and invested in a new receiver. To consolidate your seven remotes, you've plunked down another $80 on a universal controller, a device so perfectly sophisticated, it takes a sequence of seven buttons to power the TV off, cleverly ensuring that you are the only one who can use it.

MAXIM EXCEPTIONS

Something I learned at a very young age from my father. He was a genius when it came to every single gadget or appliance in the home . . . unless it was in the kitchen. There his powers failed him. For whatever reason, he simply wasn't able to help fix (or operate) the dishwasher, laundry machines, or oven. These devices confuse us men. It's baffling. And we have no desire to learn more.

MAXIM #66

YOU SEE EYE TO EYE
WITH JACK BAUER.

YOU DON'T WATCH much TV, but god damn it, Jack Bauer is a man you can relate to. Sure, maybe you have a few superficial differences: you've never tortured terrorists; you haven't (yet) assassinated a government agent to save the lives of millions; you've never died and been resurrected; your cell phone doesn't have the same never-fail service or battery power; you eat; you don't watch your family members die at CTU and then repeatedly bring *more* family members back to CTU since it's such a safe house; you sleep; you tend to wear fewer than seventeen different outfits each day; and you've never threatened to kill a U.S. president.

Other than that, it's like you're the same guy. You *get* him. You get his unwavering devotion to his values, you get his determination to complete the mission even if it means chopping off a dude's head ("I'm going to need a hacksaw"), you get the submergence of his ego.

MAXIM IN ACTION

Ten other men from television who have earned your respect:

(1.) Tony Soprano, *The Sopranos.* There's one crucial thing you love about him, it's possibly this book's most important nugget of wisdom. You love that—

(2.) George Costanza, *Seinfeld.* Couldn't you just see his reaction to being selected? "Jerry! I made the list, Jerry! *Maxims of Manhood*—MANHOOD! Who would have thought? Me! A real man? Are you kidding me? I'm bustin', Jerry, I'm bustin'!" A real man he ain't, but George is your faults personified. For an extended discussion on what Costanza means to the workplace, see MAXIM #60.

(3.) Sam Malone, *Cheers*. The one man who gets a pass on dying his hair.

(4.) Don Draper, *Mad Men*. The closest thing TV has ever seen to a walking and talking Raymond Carver short story.

(5.) Dale Cooper, *Twin Peaks*. The only man in television's history who can act like a chipper dork ("That's one damn fine cup of coffee!") but also give the impression that he could, if he chose, cut your throat by blinking.

(6.) Titus Pullo, *Rome*. You gotta love a foot soldier who cock-blocks Julius Caesar to shag Cleopatra. And when this guy wants a girl, he'll literally crush the skull of her fiancé, then seduce her, then marry her, then he'll wait a few years and murder her. The best part? He's the show's *good guy*.

(7.) Stringer Bell, *The Wire*. The best character on television's best show. Despite the fact that he sold drugs, killed innocents, and murdered his lifelong best friend.

(8.) Fox Mulder, *The X-Files*. Let's just pretend he didn't make the sequel. Or *Evolution*. Or *House of D*. Or *Full Frontal*. This guy gets stuff done, fights the system, and doesn't believe in "time management" BS (see MAXIM #52).

(9.) John Madden, *Sunday Night Football*. He'd be on the short-list for the corny "What famous person would you have dinner with?" if he wouldn't eat your entire meal.

(10.) Chuck Norris, *Walker, Texas Ranger*. A little cheesy? You bet. But a book about manhood without Chuck Norris would be like a bowl of cereal without milk. Which reminds me, when Chuck Norris eats cereal he doesn't need milk.

MAXIM EXCEPTIONS

If you've never seen *24*, then obviously you don't see eye to eye with Jack Bauer. But maybe you've seen these guys, others who make the Honorable Mention of TV Machismo: Captain Kirk, Bill Cosby, Nate Fisher, Vic Mackey, Jimmy McNulty, Al Swearengen, Jack Shephard, and Homer Simpson. And if you see eye to eye with Richard Simmons, then you should probably drop this book.

MAXIM #67

DON'T BE THAT GUY.

EVERYONE KNOWS THAT Guy. He's the scourge of nightlife, the butt of all jokes, the dregs of our gender. That Guy isn't breaking any laws, per se, but he breaks the basic rules of human decency.

When you're at the bar, you are never allowed to be That Guy. Specifically, you'll never be:

That Guy who pays for a beer with a hundred-dollar bill, flaunting it, waving it back and forth, as if women will come flocking because he's made 20 percent of what a hooker makes in an hour.

That Guy who plunks down $500 on bottle service . . . and then drinks so much he barfs in the champagne bucket. (I'm looking at you, Wes.) VIP does not, in fact, stand for Very Important Puke.

That Guy who clips his BlackBerry to his belt. You're no fashion snob, but you intuitively get that on Saturday night—or any night, really—it shouldn't look like you just came from the IT server room.

That Guy who talks on his cell phone, loudly, about his stock portfolio. He says something like, "Wait, you mean I only have ten thousand shares of IBM? Go ahead and double it."

That Guy who does the "sneak attack" to dance with girls. You've seen the move: on a crowded dance floor, the guy sneaks up to the girl from behind, and then sort of grinds against her back and forth—before she's ever even seen him—hoping that she's drunk enough not to mind.

That Guy who thinks the waitress is flirting with him (she's not) and calls her Honey and Darling, then, after the seventh beer, doesn't quite grab her ass but "accidentally" brushes his hand against her butt.

That Guy who accepts round after round of free beers, then never once buys a drink for his friends.

That Guy who tips a buck on a $30-round of beers.

That Guy who steps on his buddy's jokes and ruins a potential pickup (see MAXIM #78 on cockblocking).

MAXIM IN ACTION

If you think you might be acting like Rachel McAdams's fiancé in *Wedding Crashers,* chances are you've turned into That Guy. If you're acting like just about any of Carrie's dates in *Sex and the City,* you've turned into That Guy. If you're actually familiar with Carrie's dates in *Sex and the City,* you've turned into Another Guy altogether. See MAXIM #66 on TV shows.

MAXIM EXCEPTIONS

Everybody has an off-night. Sometimes you forget to tip. Sometimes you get drunker than Lindsay Lohan on a postrehab binge. Sometimes you really *need* to talk about your stock portfolio and you can't muffle your voice. Fine. One violation does not a That Guy make. Just don't develop a pattern of overall nightlife douchebaggery.

MAXIM #68

NO CHITCHATTING AT THE MOVIES.

WATCHING A MOVIE isn't that hard, really. It's a simple process. (1) Turn on the movie. (2) Sit on the couch. (3) Watch the movie. That's it. In the grand mechanics of life's activities, it's pretty low on the scale of complexity.

You can handle this three-step process. Many women can't. In the middle of *Heat*'s diner scene between Pacino and De Niro, for instance, she'll wonder why Pacino had a spiked haircut in *Godfather III*, and then she'll laugh and try and visualize you with a spike, then she'll say that, while we're on the subject, maybe you should change your sideburns and start using pomade. Pomade? You don't know what that is. She pulls out her laptop to show you, and the next thing you know, Val Kilmer's dead.

You rewind the movie and watch the scene again. She sits silent for twenty seconds, then wonders if De Niro's worst movie was *Analyze That* or *The Fan* . . . which gets her going on the unfortunate career of Wesley Snipes—how could someone with so much talent make so much trash? What happened to him? Wasn't he *amazing* in *Waiting to Exhale?* You tell her you've never seen that movie and she says *you've never SEEN that movie?!* and the next thing you know, Val Kilmer's dead.

Figure 7.8. *Fill your mouth with this, not words.*

MAXIM IN ACTION

Like most of life, movies are meant to be enjoyed in silence (see MAXIM #68). Two other activities you wish would be quieter:

Driving. It's calming—therapeutic, even—to focus on the road, relax, and immerse yourself in the blather of talk radio. She asks why you can listen to the idiotic hosts of a talk show but won't listen to her, your wife, the woman you say you love. You say you can't hear her—the radio's too loud.

Watching sports. Yes, there might be 162 baseball games a season, but a W in April is just as important as a W in September. You'll have more time for chitchat after the baseball season. You promise. She considers this, frowns, and then says that after the baseball season, doesn't football start? You say it does. As does basketball—which ends in June, just in time for baseball. You tell her not to worry, there are two days a year that have no major sports games: the days before and after the MLB All-Star game. (The NFL, NBA, and NHL are all in off-season.) Those two days will be special, you promise, devoted just to the relationship and nothing else. Except the home run derby.

MAXIM EXCEPTIONS

During the movie, you're outraged at interruptions for gossip, celebrity trivia, or substantive conversation about real life . . . but you'll gleefully pause the sucker to point out some arcane bit of trivia that you and only you are aware of. Usually this involves guns. In *Platoon*, for example, you'll stop the movie thirteen times to point out that when you fire the M-16A2, it's best to focus on the front-sight post, not the real aperture. You'll repeat this a few times. She'll ask if you think Charlie Sheen's marriage to Brooke Allen will last. You shh-hhhh her . . . you're watching the movie, after all.

MAXIM #69

NEVER WATCH A SHOW WITH "DANCING" IN THE TITLE.

NO *DANCING WITH the Stars*. No *So You Think You Can Dance*. No *Dancing with the Millionaires* or *Who Wants to Wear a Leotard?* For the sake of argument, let's think about what you could possibly find interesting about these shows:

The outfits: The only outfits you find interesting—ever—are the costumes on Halloween, and that's because your coworkers, in the most glorious of all holiday traditions, think it's appropriate to dress like strippers.

The celebrities: This is the ultimate betrayal. Seeing Jerry Rice and Emmitt Smith doing the cha-cha-cha is more appalling than watching OJ Simpson turn into a killer, Mike Tyson turn into an ear muncher, or Tom Cruise turn into a couch-jumping Scientologist. Homicide and intolerance are one thing, but at least those guys never lost their sense of decorum.

The choreography: Much like window treatments (see MAXIM #47), you should have only the vaguest notion of the meaning of the word "choreography," much less how it works or what makes it magical. You know its meaning in the context of fight scenes—*Crouching Tiger, Hidden Dragon*, for instance, has well-choreographed swordfights—but you'd never whistle and say, "Boy! Look at those staircase turns. Just look at 'em!"

The dancing itself: As established in MAXIM #61, dancing is only a means to an end. The only thing worse than dancing is *watching another man dance*. It has the same entertainment value as watching another man put on his deodorant, Q-tip the wax out of his ears, or grimace through a violent case of diarrhea. Then again, who knows. Next season, Fox could premiere "Who Wants to Watch a Man Put On Deodorant!" and it'd still get more viewers than *Mad Men*.

MAXIM IN ACTION

In addition to shows on dancing, the following must also be avoided: *The Hills* (unless it's a sweeps week episode where Lauren Conrad hooks up with Heidi Montag); anything on Lifetime or Oxygen; *Desperate Housewives* (this is less about gender and more about taste . . . not that I would know); or *Ugly Betty.* You're not exactly sure what the premise of *Ugly Betty* is—something about how a woman's character, spirit, and inner beauty are more important than superficial looks—but you find it unsettling and you avoid it.

MAXIM EXCEPTIONS

Here we have a conflict. An absolute "No *Dancing with the Stars*" doesn't square with MAXIM #87: "Being considerate doesn't make you a wimp." 87 wins. If your girlfriend cajoles you into watching one of these shows, fine, this is your compromise, your penance, your way of acting like a reasonable person. But don't enjoy yourself. Mock. And act like you do when two of your football rivals play each other: root for injuries.

LEARN TO MIX THE FIVE COCKTAILS.

IT STARTS WITH the equipment. After college graduation, every man's residence must be stocked with a martini shaker, blender, measuring device (the little spoons are optional; the jigger is not), cutting board, martini glasses, highball glasses, and a lint brush. This last has nothing to do with alcohol. It's just a good thing to have.

Once you have the right tools and the right booze, you must know how to make the five most important cocktails: the princess drink, the tough-girl drink, the man's drink, the perfect Bloody Mary, and the superior martini.

MAXIM IN ACTION

The Princess Drink

You might be shocked to hear this, but all women are not the same. There are two kinds: princesses and tough girls. Therefore your bag of tricks must include at least one cocktail for the princess, and one cocktail for the tough girl. Princess drinks include apple martinis, mai tais, any drink with a prefix before "tini" like chocotini or pink-and-sweet-tini, and anything frozen.

The Tough-Girl Drink

As with every category, it's not necessary to know how to make *all* of these drinks, but you must master one from each. The Tough-Girl drink is a harder one to crack. It's less froofy but still a touch feminine: gimlets, manhattans, Tom Collinses, whiskey sours, Long Island ice teas, sidecars, and the like.

The Man's Drink

A drink's masculinity is directly proportional to the likelihood that when a small child tastes it, he will vomit. These are strong and dangerous and disgusting. These drinks are your profile in courage: Gibsons, anything brown and bitter on the rocks, old-fashioneds, rusty nails, and anything neat.

Figure 7.10. *Lunch.*

The Perfect Bloody Mary

Yes, it needs to have real celery. No, it can't be made with V8. Be sure to incorporate Worcestershire sauce, Tabasco sauce, black pepper, horseradish, a wedge of lemon, and for hair of the dog—a chaser of two Advils.

The Superior Martini

You should know that "shaken, not stirred" is bunk. A proper gin martini is stirred, not shaken. A better ode to the martini, courtesy of James Thurber: "One martini is all right. Two are too many, and three are not enough."

MAXIM EXCEPTIONS

If you don't drink, no one expects you to be a magician behind the bar. That being said . . . if you *don't* drink, you get even more points for cocktail wizardry. Think Sam Malone from *Cheers*. Or take my buddy Kabir. He's never swallowed an ounce of alcohol, but he keeps a well-stocked liquor cabinet, he knows how to pair wines, and you're damn right he can make one drink from each of the five categories.

PART VIII.
BUDDIES

MAXIM #71

YOU CAN HANDLE SILENCE.

THE MARK OF a great friendship is the ability to treat your friend like a total stranger. When you go on a road trip with your best friend, you can make it from Chicago to Boston without breaking the 100-word barrier.

You can handle silence. You embrace it. Silence lets you reflect on the important things in life, like whether the Lakers overpaid their second-round draft pick. Silence lets you get in touch with your feelings, like whether you need to readjust your balls.

Silence means confidence. Self-assurance. You're comfortable in your own skin. You don't need to broadcast your intelligence, and you silently laugh at those who do. Silence doesn't signal tension; it signals mutual respect.

In the company of women, however, your silence has been known to create awkwardness. Let's pretend you're having a late-night, post-coital, pillow-talky conversation before bed. She has just asked where this relationship is going. She says that she loves you. She wants to know that it's for real.

At this fragile moment, you understand, correctly, that the last thing to do is open your mouth and spoil the night's magic. So you look deep in her eyes but say nothing. You caress her hair, press her body close. She repeats herself. You kiss her forehead and wonder if you remembered to set your Fantasy Football lineup (see MAXIM #12). She says that she's never felt this way before. You wonder if the guns on Batman's bat-pod violate his no-killing policy.

She says that she's serious. Finally you look at her—not exactly sure what she's been talking about—and you say, "Me too." Her body unclenches in delight.

You both go to sleep happy.

MAXIM IN ACTION

I have a buddy named Gut. He's like Silent Bob from the Kevin Smith movies—you know the guy. He'll say nothing for the entire weekend, simply nodding his head, raising an eyebrow, occasionally emoting with a nice, long sigh. He's almost as communicative as a dog, grunting his approval or displeasure. When he's hungry he'll eat; when he's thirsty he'll drink.

Gut served as best man for our buddy Eric's wedding. At the reception we were all a little worried. Could Gut give a toast? Would he simply pick up his champagne, nod at Eric and Heather, grunt some, then blurt out in raw caveman: "Eric GOOOOD!!! Heather GOOODDD!!! Wedding GOOOODD!!! Fire BAADDDD!!!!"

We drank. And waited nervously. Then drank more. Then Gut took a page straight out of the Silent Bob playbook: he delivered, hands down, the most articulate toast any of us had ever heard. He was funny and poignant and touching. Gut's legacy? Silence doesn't mean you have nothing to say. It means you say something only when it matters.

MAXIM EXCEPTIONS

There is one occasion when silence between buddies can actually be uncomfortable: watching sex scenes. If two grown men are together in a dark room, sitting side by side on the couch, it's just a little weird to watch *9½ Weeks*. During the film's erotic moments, the proper protocol is to loudly, crudely, boisterously comment on the actress's "skills" and "merits" as a performer.

MAXIM #72

NEVER ASK ANOTHER MAN
HOW YOU LOOK.

REMEMBER "THE JIMMY," the classic *Seinfeld* episode? Elaine asks George whether he thinks a guy's good looking. George stammers. Elaine presses. George blushes and refuses to answer. Elaine says, "Just because you admit another man is good looking doesn't mean you're homosexual."

George glares at her. He growls, "It doesn't help."

For better or worse, a straight man is not allowed to tell another straight man that he looks good. It could start a fight. It could ruin a friendship. You can't comment on another man's shoes, jacket, shirt, and certainly not the cut of his jeans.

In fact, you must pretend that your male friends look identical. It's a miracle you can tell them apart. Mostly you use voice recognition. And height. You can tell which of your friends are short or tall.

Three words that one man should never say to another: "You smell good." For one, he doesn't. He probably smells like sweat and feet and gas. This is how men smell. And even if he *does* smell magnificent—a cocktail of manly spice and clean, warm musk, like he's fresh from the barbershop—wait, stop right there. He doesn't smell like that. He just *doesn't*. And if you think he does, think again, and wonder what it says about you.

Unless he did something extraordinary like dyed his hair green, you shouldn't mention your buddy's haircut. You shouldn't even notice it. If you do, it's to give him shit for getting a spectacularly awful bowl cut, telling him he looks like Javier Bardem in *No Country for Old Men*.

Compare this to women. Girls can actually meet other girls in a bar—complete strangers—and say something like, "Love your bag!" and become fast friends. They compliment each other's lipstick. Perfume. They can even sort of flirt. A rational person might ask,

"Doesn't this demonstrate that women are more enlightened, more tolerant, less insecure, less homophobic, more comfortable in their own skin?"

You chuckle at this nonsense. You know it means they're bi-curious.

MAXIM IN ACTION

Let's imagine an emphatically heterosexual scenario. You're about to go on a date. With a girl. You consider a few different shirts (this may take no longer than fifteen seconds) and finally settle on one that's kinda fitted. And let's say your roommate is home watching TV. You are forbidden from interrupting his game and asking, "Do I look okay in this shirt?" Even though the root driver of this question is the heterosexual pursuit of heterosexual sex—you just put your buddy in an impossible, untenable position.

MAXIM EXCEPTIONS

For some reason that defies any conventional explanation, you are allowed to ask another guy if he's "been lifting," say that he "looks big," and ask him if he's been working out. It makes utterly no sense. Even though you've clearly just sized up his body—took in his pecs, checked out his biceps—you're just engaging in a little manly, rah-rah gym talk. But if you ask him where he got his shoes? You're a queen. Not that there's anything . . .

MAXIM #73

KEEP OPRAH OUT OF
THE BACHELOR PARTY.

NO OPRAH, NO feelings, no emotions, no discussions of relationships. No phone calls to the girlfriends or wives. Think of the weekend as a healthy "trust test" for you and your loved one. If you call during the bachelor party, your relationship fails. As a corollary, girlfriends, wives, babies, and children should never be discussed or even *mentioned.* For this weekend they simply don't exist.

That's the first of the Five Rules of Bachelor Parties. The others:

No pictures. It's pretty straightforward. Pictures mean Facebook. Facebook means divorce. Which, for many people, is bad.

Quarantine Maury. Every group has a guy like "Maury." The weird dude no one really likes, the one who's a friend of a friend of a friend of a friend, the one who got invited by accident, the one who concludes a toast with "So Say We All." Someone's gotta take the bullet. Keep Maury away from the groom.

Figure 8.3. *The only girlfriends allowed.*

No girls can be invited. It doesn't matter if she's the groom's best platonic-girlfriend from kindergarten. It doesn't matter if she's a lesbian.

Unless he gets greedy with the lap dances, the groom never pays.

MAXIM IN ACTION

Confession time. Montreal. My buddy Stephane's bachelor party. We were at a greasy diner, bacon-egg-and-cheesing our way through a collective hangover. So far so good; the night before, we'd showered the groom with steaks and lap dances and Grey Goose. We drank our coffee silently, recouping, mustering strength for the next strip club, which we planned to hit by 11 A.M.

Everyone at the table—Erik, Kabir, Adam, Wes, Omer—had a serious girlfriend, so they were especially grateful for the weekend of bro-and-ho time. Which leads to my faux pas. Chewing a mouthful of eggs I blurted out, "So who's next? Let's lay odds on who's next to get married." Silence. Disbelief. Shock. Then shaking heads and disappointment.

How bad was this? How grave a sin? If our bachelor party were a Catholic Church, it would be the same as marching to the altar, snacking communion wafers like Doritos, ripping the Bible into sheets and folding them into little origami hats, and licking a body shot of holy water off a nun.

MAXIM EXCEPTIONS

Your role as "drunken debauchery enabler" has limits. There's a very clear line: you shouldn't push your buddy so far that he cheats.

Witness the sad case of a guy I know—let's call him by the pseudonym "Barry," as the anecdote would terminate his marriage. At Barry's Miami bachelor party, his friends stuffed his liver with tequila and ushered him to the strip club. They goaded him into a "private dance." They gave the stripper a wad of cash and told her to make it special.

In the private room she got buck naked, pumping up and down on Barry's lap. She unzipped his jeans, teasing, playful, stroking his boxers. Still bobbing up and down, and in one slick motion before he could react—so claims Barry—she yanked his boxers to the side and mounted him, full penetration, sans condom. Barry yelped in surprise. He bolted from the room, ordered a double shot of vodka, hit the bathroom, then poured the vodka all over his penis, thinking it would cleanse any STDs.

The moral? When the groom gets as shit-faced as Barry, it's your responsibility to monitor him, corral him, keep him pure(ish) for his wedding. On the bright side, Barry's happily married, he doesn't have any diseases, and (probably) doesn't have any kids.

MAXIM #74

NEVER ASK TO "SEE PICTURES."

CONFESSION TIME. I once broke this rule. Over the phone, my buddy Eric told me about his trip to Italy. I said what I thought sounded reasonable: "Sounds amazing. I'd love to see the pictures."

Long pause. When he finally spoke, I could feel his disappointment and disgust: "Pictures? *Pictures?*" (He sounded a little like Jim Mora saying "Playoffs?!") Another long pause and then he said, "No, man. That's what girls do."

Eric's right. Pictures are not to be shared between men. I immediately apologized and retracted the question. We said our goodbyes, both shaken and embarrassed.

It's not that men don't give a damn about each other's experiences. We do. But there's a certain code in how we communicate. Fawning over photo albums—like old ladies sipping tea—tramples this protocol.

If, through some cockamamie fluke of circumstances, two men are leafing through photographs together, they should do so as swiftly and joylessly as possible. You don't linger. You don't lovingly caress the photographs, marveling at the lighting or the wonderful use of shadows. You don't use the word "adorable."

MAXIM IN ACTION

A different buddy, Evan, once asked if I wanted to see pictures of his 1-year-old daughter. He had his digital camera right there. What am I gonna say, no? So despite this breach of decorum, there I was—at a *bachelor party!*—staring over Evan's shoulder, gawking at baby pictures.

Not only did Evan lose points for introducing babies to a bachelor party (for more on this, see MAXIM #73), he created a serious problem. As he showed me picture after picture of his little daughter, I had utterly no clue what to say. I was literally speechless. "She's cute" sounded pervy, "She has your eyes" was equally preposterous, so I stuck with vapid comments like "Huh" and "Nice." Then I worried that I didn't sound supportive enough, so at the final picture, I said, "That's a great shot. Can I have that one?"

Oops. Evan looked at me and said, "You want to *have* this picture of my daughter? What, are you a sicko?" He was clearly joking (to this day, in fact, he maintains an uncomfortable running joke that I'm a pedophile), but it wasn't our finest moment.

Who's at fault here? Evan or me? Both. It was a clumsy comment on my part, but the fact is that men *don't have the vocabulary* for baby-pictures talk; therefore, it must be avoided altogether.

MAXIM EXCEPTIONS

Digital photos may be sent over e-mail or shared online. This lets the receiver view them as quickly as possible—or not at all—sparing all parties any awkwardness.

There are some pictures that you're encouraged to share. If you have an incriminating picture of your friend that involves public nudity, vomit, or anything that could get him imprisoned, this should be distributed to as many friends as possible. These are all Kodak moments.

MAXIM #75

A BUDDY'S FIGHT IS YOUR FIGHT.

TRUE FRIENDSHIP DEMANDS blind stupidity. Without knowing the circumstances, the causes, or who's right and who's wrong, you must follow your friend into battle. You don't have time to think. You're not allowed to think. You're only allowed to hit the guy he's hitting.

Your buddy could be wrong (he probably is). He could be drunk (he certainly is). Unprovoked, he could have sucker-punched a guy in the nose. It doesn't matter. As far as you're concerned, the innocent guy just stole your wallet, plunged his tongue down your girlfriend's throat, and took a dump on Grandma's grave.

Figure 8.5. *Have your buddy's back.*

This doesn't mean you're an instigator. If you can squash the fight before it happens, fine; your buddy will thank you later. Careful though. Remember your allegiance. In your role as negotiator, you may not apologize for your friend; your buddy has the moral high ground—always—even if he vomited in the dude's cowboy hat. You may not back down . . . even if they're bigger, meaner, and tatooier.

A slightly more complicated scenario: what if two of your friends are fighting each other? Tricky. It's a judgment call. The conventional wisdom is to break things up; we're all friends, right? Cooler heads and all that junk. And if your intra-friend brawl is simply the result of too much alcohol—with no real underlying beef—that's probably the way to go.

Alternatively, the tough-love approach is to let your friends wail it out. It's the guys' version of therapy. If your friends have a bottled-up, multiyear feud, now is the time to uncork. Let them emote with their fists.

MAXIM IN ACTION

You don't have to be a particularly effective fighter. In fact, let's not kid ourselves. When you say you're going to "kick this guy's ass," what you really mean is, "I'm gonna get maybe a few feet closer to the guy, ask him if he 'wants some of this'—whatever 'this' is—and then we'll both awkwardly stare at each other. If things really heat up, I might say, 'Come on!' and then he'll say 'Come on!' and then we'll keep saying that, incrementally louder each time, until people step in and shove us apart." And that's fine; 99 percent of the time, all you need is puffy swagger. The other 1 percent, all you need is good health insurance.

MAXIM EXCEPTIONS

It's best to avoid a police report. If your friend is clearly winning the fight and he won't stop, don't pile on. But don't watch from the sidelines, either; your role has morphed into that of peacekeeper. Don't let him pummel his opponent like Edward Norton bloodying Angel Face in *Fight Club*. Unless the opponent actually is Jared Leto, in which case, let him wail away.

MAXIM #76

MASTER THE BRO-HUG.

A GENERATION AGO, when our fathers said hello to their friends, they kept the maximum possible open space between their two bodies. They shook hands without even bending their elbows—the straighter the arm, the straighter the orientation.

Times have changed. If you shake hands with the Frankenstein stiff-arm, you get weird looks and open mockery. The old-school handshake is for job interviews, defense lawyers, potential fathers-in-law, and trench coat–wearing police detectives who just want to ask you a few questions. It means you don't trust the man. You don't like him.

The handshake has evolved (devolved?) into an elaborate, awkward, yet-to-be-fully-codified bro-hug. Nobody is sure how it works. It's part handshake, part hug, part back pat, part shoulder clasp. There's no surefire way to do it right. But there are several ways to do it wrong:

- The bro-hug may never be chest to chest, which runs the risk of being crotch to crotch. Keep your bodies at a thirty-five-degree angle. You have botched the maneuver if you can smell his aftershave, feel his breath, or accidentally end up face to face making close, unsettling eye contact.
- When you bro-hug your buddy, keep your hands moving with vigorous, brisk, heterosexual purpose. Your hands shouldn't linger. Stay in motion. Practice the "three-pat back clap": in mid-bro-hug, thump his back three times as a cadence for "I'm! [thump] Not! [thump] Gay! [thump]."
- It should last only seven seconds, preferably fewer. In fact, think of it more as an extended "chest bump," taking care not to actually bump chests, which violates the above.
- Something else to avoid—while it was cute during season one of *Entourage*, saying, "Let's hug it out, bitch!" is a joke that has long overstayed its welcome.

MAXIM IN ACTION

The etiquette is most baffling for friends you kinda know but not really. Do you execute the half-hug? Go with the Frankenstein? The same goes for coworkers and business partners you only see sporadically at the office, awkwardly debating the BCS rankings. For these unpleasant encounters, conventional wisdom suggests something in between the handshake and the bro-hug . . . a shake followed by an elbow tap. When in doubt, let the other guy initiate contact.

MAXIM EXCEPTIONS

Another way to go is the aggressive, over-the-top "bear hug," which violates every one of the rules, but it's still considered (mostly) appropriate in certain circumstances. It must be reserved for an extraordinarily good friend—or brother, maybe—you haven't seen in at least sixteen months. You should charge your friend like he's a running back and you're a linebacker, violently colliding your bodies and crushing your spines. It's okay to grab and hold. For this audacious maneuver, for this lifelong friend of yours, the goal is to crash into him with so much force, so much raw power, that if he weighed an ounce less he'd crumple to the floor and die.

MAXIM #77

SUPPORT YOUR FRIEND'S CRAPPY BAND.

YOUR BUDDY'S BAND could be a cross between Richard Marx and the Jonas Brothers. Or maybe he just bangs a wooden bowl against the ground, over and over, chanting monosyllabic lyrics—*Ugh! Hut! Ugh! Hut!*—as the bowl strikes the ground, and he calls this one-man band "Bowl on Ground." He's not being ironic. He's not making a joke. He simply loves the rhythmic, pulsing beats of a bowl banging against the ground, and he suspects that others love it, too.

As his friend, it is your sacred duty to go see Bowl on Ground. Yes, that means paying a cover charge. Yes, that means dragging a couple of other friends along. Yes, that means forking over ten bucks for an EP you'll never play. And after the show, that means looking him dead in the eye and saying, "Hey man. You killed it. That bowl really hit the ground."

MAXIM IN ACTION

In addition to seeing Bowl on Ground, you are required to help your buddy with the following unpleasant activities:

Help him move. Unless you barely know the guy (like Keith Hernandez in the classic *Seinfeld* episode), you are required to give him fourteen hours of back-breaking work on a Saturday, and he is required to feed you a soggy slice of pizza.

Read his writing. If he has some misguided notion of being a writer, he'll probably ask you to read his wretched short stories. (Guilty.) This puts you in an awkward spot. You can't tell him that his stories suck, he sucks, and that he should stick to coding Java. But you can't blow smoke up his ass, either. Be encouraging, be honest, and follow the feedback model: "I really liked the [sorta miserable thing that didn't suck as much as the rest of the story], but I thought [wretched cliché that made you want to barf all over his shitty manuscript] could use just a little work."

Give him a lift to the airport or hospital. Unless he abuses this privilege with a gauntlet of flights. You're a buddy, not a cabbie.

Help him with the occasional home-improvement chore. This doesn't include the basics like mowing the lawn or weeding. But if there's an extraordinary home-improvement project that requires a second set of hands, you are required to haul Sheetrock, mix cement, or lug around cinderblocks. (Note: The big stuff goes without saying, like bailing him out of prison or talking him down from a convincing tranny.)

MAXIM EXCEPTIONS

While you're obligated to support your buddy's band, you are not required to be a groupie. If he plays every week and expects you to support him each and every time, you have a right to draw the line. He'll understand. There's only so many times you can see the bowl clang against the ground.

Figure 8.7. *You don't have to go as far as becoming a groupie.*

MAXIM #78

COCKBLOCK AND DIE.

SOMETIMES IT'S SIMPLE. If your buddy's flirting with the blonde at the bar, it's obviously unacceptable for you to swoop in, box him out like you're getting a rebound, and hijack the conversation. But cockblocking can be subtler. Trickier. Sometimes the rules of the game are less clearly defined.

There are three murky areas:

#1 Not-Quite-Sloppy Seconds

Let's say your buddy strikes out with the girl (probably not a stretch) and this same girl is clearly interested in you (a stretch). What then? Permission hinges on two variables: (1) how much your friend likes her; (2) securing his blessing. If your friend's all gooey for her—fawning and crushing like Ben Stiller in *There's Something about Mary*—then she's off-limits. Period. There are millions of other girls. Sure, there are also millions of potential buddies, too, but they're harder to replace.

#2 Gross Incompetence

Cockblocking doesn't have to be malicious. It's possible that your friends are so verbally clumsy, so artless, that they'll trample any encounter (like James, later). So what's the workaround? Like any good coach, you should know your personnel. You wouldn't have your center guarding the point guard, so you shouldn't have your marble-mouthed friends play wing. When you're one-on-one with a girl at the bar, it should be understood that the two of you are to be left alone.

#3 Dibs Ambiguity

It's not always clear who has dibs. What if you both meet the girl at the same time? Or what if it's three guys, three girls, and there's geographic confusion over who matches up with whom? As discussed in MAXIM #81 on the "wedge," the guy who makes contact gets dibs.

Absent that, unless there's some prearranged agreement, boldness counts. Whoever initiates conversation gets dibs, and has dibs for the rest of the night.

MAXIM IN ACTION

The first thing you should know about my buddy James: he talks in the deepest voice you've ever heard. It makes everything he says funny. He could give a eulogy and we'd all crack up. James is the cockblocker par excellence. He's not ignorant, he's just clueless. You could talk to a girl for three hours and James would swagger up to her and say in his deep, white-Darth-Vader voice, "I'm James" and stare at her, silent, as if waiting for applause . . . and the girl leaves in confusion. One time we went on a double date. After a few rounds of drinks we're all dancing, and then he awkwardly grabs both the girls' shoulders—to clarify, this is *not* smooth, this is *not* daring charisma, the girls are weirded out—and says in his deep baritone, "What do you say we see a little *lesbian* action," then tries to smoosh their heads together. And thus ends the date. Everyone has a buddy like James—great guy, means well, but womanizing kryptonite.

MAXIM EXCEPTIONS

If you've been cockblocked, it's acceptable (and encouraged) to get revenge through a payback cockblock. It's like when a pitcher intentionally hits a batter: sometimes retaliation is justified. Additionally, unless they're clearly on a date or he's been with the girl for hours, it's acceptable to cockblock strangers. You don't make the rules. You just play by them.

MAXIM #79

NO POKING ON FACEBOOK.

YEARS AGO YOU heard about Facebook. And your first thought was, "Isn't this for high school cheerleaders, and is it really age-appropriate, or gender-appropriate, or not-being-a-tool-appropriate for you to set up a virtual account to virtually communicate with virtual friends with whom you have virtually nothing in common? What about this is appealing?"

So you hedged. You stalled. You ignored the trend. You kept deleting those irritating "Invitations to Join Facebook" from buddies who should know better.

Then at some point you caved. You realized that, hell, when even your *parents* are joining Facebook, you could put it off no longer. You signed up. And that's fine. You haven't violated a maxim . . . yet. You must observe the following rules of Facebook:

No poking. You shouldn't poke a guy. You shouldn't poke a girl. You shouldn't poke anyone. In fact, not even the billionaire inventors of Facebook understand the purpose of poking, why it's in the system, or what message you could possibly be trying to convey. When girls poke, it looks juvenile. When guys poke, it looks either juvenile or smarmy or both.

No blind-friend requests. There are many ways to meet women. It's fine to stalk them at the bar or awkwardly approach them when buying cantaloupe at the grocery store, but seeing a cute photo and "friending" her—with absolutely no real-life introduction—is gross and weaselly.

Figure 8.9. *It's okay to stalk a woman anywhere but online.*

No excessive comments on photos. That's just weird. It looks like you're trolling your friends. Keep your comments, at a maximum, to one photo per album.

No posting anything you'll regret. Theoretically, Facebook has privacy settings that enable you to shelter your photos, videos, and embarrassing confessions from public searches or certain friends. Don't trust them. Don't set your status update to "Greg again has that burning sensation, and his urine is slightly mango colored." Also, Greg should know better. Mango? See MAXIM #2.

MAXIM IN ACTION

Another key violation of Facebook guy etiquette: Limit your applications. Some of them are fun. The "Movie Compatibility Test" is a pleasant enough ten-minute time waster and serves as a nice intro to Facebook. Same with "iLike" and a few others. But avoid clutter. Never cram your page with nineteen apps like "My Favorite Flavors of Bubblegum" and "What Does Your Soul Smell Like?"

MAXIM EXCEPTIONS

Heavier Facebook usage is actually encouraged for out-of-town friends, as it helps you follow a more important principle: you don't like talking on the phone. When used properly, you can (kind of) stay in touch with 130 friends in just a few simple keystrokes. Who needs actual companionship, deep conversations, and quality bonding when you can skim a seven-second status update?

MAXIM #80

HAVE AT LEAST ONE VERY GOOD GAY FRIEND.

YOU MUST HAVE at least one very good gay friend. Or at least one very gay good friend. What's that? All your friends are straight? Here's a secret: they're not. Sooner or later, one of them will come out and you'll have your quota.

Back in the late '90s, thanks to *My Best Friend's Wedding* and *Will and Grace*, it became chic to think of the gay man as "every straight girl's best accessory." Things have changed. Intelligent straight men have now adopted this theory as our own, leveraging their gayness to amplify our straightness.

Skeptical? Benefits include:

Unparalleled female reconnaissance. Your gay friends have a unique ability to ferret out deep, embarrassing secrets from otherwise shy women. Gay men get the juiciest stories; they're harmless and therefore trustworthy: talk to them, learn from them, spy with them.

Fashion wisdom. True, you despise shopping (see MAXIM #42), but your gay friend will let you streamline the entire process, telling you precisely what to buy and where to get it. Don't be skittish because of his own wardrobe choices: he's savvy enough to make recommendations both straight and stylish.

Candor. Unlike your girlfriend or even your platonic friend-girls (there really needs to be a word for that), your gay friends can call you out with brutal candor. They can tell you when you're starting to look fat. When your hairline needs help. When your biceps look flabby. No one else in your life, really, offers the same kind of unfettered honesty.

175

Workout tips. He can probably beat you up, and he probably looks better than you do naked. Don't be embarrassed by this. Learn from it. Let him give you some workout pointers.

Picking up women. Try it. When you go to a bar with your gay friend, you're immediately (albeit subconsciously) perceived by women as more interesting, more substantive, more open-minded. Just don't get *too* close with him in public or else you'll risk the perception of, well, you know.

MAXIM IN ACTION

Your gay friend also provides the "Get out of intolerance free card." You know all those off-color, insensitive, politically incorrect jokes you just told? Just talk about your gay friends and you're off the hook. Say, for a wildly implausible, completely theoretical example, you wrote a book with ninety-nine essays that all have the faint whiff of homophobia, even though it's absolutely unintended and you're actually open-minded and regret being offensive. As long as you have one positive essay about your gay friend—which also mucks around in stereotypes, might be considered offensive, and represents only 1 percent of the book—you're in the clear. Just a theoretical example.

MAXIM EXCEPTIONS

If you really don't have any gay friends—or if you simply haven't met anyone who's gay—okay, not much you can do about that. You're not expected to troll gay bars cruising for platonic gay buddies. (Funny visual though.) But you must be open-minded. Much of this book might be mistaken as homophobia—that's the risk assumed by any "real man" treatise—but that's not the intent. Just the opposite. A real man is secure enough in his sexuality—regardless of what it is—that he's not squeamish.

And it's time. Let's address the elephant in the room: yes, these maxims all (mostly) assume you're straight, but obviously a "real man" can be "real gay." But that's a different book written by a different guy. The point is this: if you're straight, you're understandably protective about your masculinity and your orientation, but you're also progressive, tolerant, and quick to embrace anyone (worthy) as your friend—regardless of their sexuality, race, creed, yada yada. And that's that.

PART IX.
WOMEN REVISITED

MAXIM #81

KNOW HOW TO WEDGE.

WE'RE ALL FAMILIAR with Maverick and Goose; we all know the tired rules about "never leaving your wingman." Obvious stuff. Kid stuff. I don't have to tell you that.

Being a good partner in crime, however, requires more finesse then simply never leaving your wingman. That's necessary but insufficient. A better test: you must know how to "wedge," and when it's your turn, you must wedge.

To understand the wedge, we must first appreciate the challenges, opportunities, and frustrations caused by the dreaded "defensive girl huddle." Girls love to do this. They order their apple martinis and cluster together, facing each other in a circle, shoulder to shoulder, chatting, forming a perfumed huddle of skirts and skin. It's the most basic formation in the girl playbook—think of it as the 4–3 defense.

The huddle intimidates. It keeps their backs to the guys, making conversation more difficult and more of a risk. It's one thing to chat her up when she's ordering a drink—you're both facing each other, you're both on the same team, rolling eyes at the bartender—but the stakes are higher when they ward you off with one big collective, circular ass.

You need a point of entry. You need a wedge. The wedge has to somehow split the defense, which requires bold action and some quick thinking on your feet. As soon as you speak, all five girls will turn to stare at you—judging—so your opening better not suck. It's a lot of pressure. (Happily, this pressure can be relieved with alcohol.)

Once the wedge makes contact—prying open the huddle—the buddies can flank the sides and chat with her friends, adding confusion, unleashing anarchy. Soon their barriers are broken, and the two groups become one.

So who's job is it to wedge? Everyone's. Mix it up. Take turns. Just as you rotate buying rounds, you should rotate being the wedge. If worse comes to worst, it's always entertaining to see your buddies humiliated and emasculated. That's what friendship's all about.

MAXIM IN ACTION

No pickup lines. Please. Save yourself and your target the embarrassment. Instead? The best wedge technique is to employ the tactic of "coconspirator." Create the illusion that you have some secret, shared agenda; that you're allies; that you have a common enemy. The common enemy could be a loud shrieking bachelorette party, it could be the slow bartender, it could be the frat boys chugging Buds and smashing cans against their foreheads (see MAXIM #63 on beer chugging). All it takes is something simple, like pointing at the loud group of girls with penis whistles and say, "Okay, *tell me* you're not part of that bachelorette party cliché?" Mockery. It's what brings the world together.

MAXIM EXCEPTIONS

What if you're in a relationship? What if you're married? Nope. You're not off the hook. In fact, this is the perfect and harmless way for you to flirt. You're the perfect wedge. You're safe. Since you have a wife, you're immediately less threatening; you can distract them while the true danger (your buddies) maneuvers for the kill. This gives you the illusion that you're still one of the guys.

MAXIM #82

GIVE VALENTINE'S DAY THE RESPECT IT DESERVES.

YOU'RE FORBIDDEN FROM looking forward to Valentine's Day. If you ever met Cupid, you'd sock him in the face and ask him why he wears diapers and looks so creepy.

You don't get it. You smell a paradox. If the soul of romance is spontaneity, and February 14 is precisely as "spontaneous" as filing your federal income tax, wouldn't that make the holiday, by definition, the least romantic day of the year?

It's all downside, no upside. If you drop the ball, you're in the doghouse. If you slog through the pageantry—roses, candles, reservations at the chic new sushi place—you're just meeting expectations, treading water, not getting credit for all the expense and hassle.

You'd be more open to Valentine's Day if our society mixed it up, did a girls' version on the even years and a guys' version on the odds. What would the guys' version look like? She asks what you want as a gift, and you tell her you'd love something special, something from the heart: the magical "gift of silence." Dinner would be delivery—a bacon-cheeseburger with a bucket of tater-tots. As for romance, you'd like Game 7 of the playoffs. Instead of buying her flowers, you buy more RAM for her laptop.

It's a Catch-22. Taking her to a nice restaurant, buying her gifts, and showering her with roses would actually *mean* something if it happened on any other day of the year. You explain this to her, and she argues that it *doesn't* happen on any other day of the year. She clearly doesn't get it.

And when Valentine's Day pops up when you just started dating the girl? Nightmare. If you do too much, you're slapped with the label of boyfriend; if you do too little, she's insulted. You can't win. (Your best bet, incidentally, is to get her a gag-gift that references an earlier conversation; this way you don't totally ignore the elephant in the room, but you don't come off as too schmaltzy too soon.)

MAXIM IN ACTION

A sneakier challenge . . . the "Valentine's Day Trap." Some girls will tell you, "I *hate* Valentine's Day. It's such a cheesy Hallmark holiday." This is what they claim. Flash-forward to February 14. When you don't bring her flowers, chocolates, or gifts—having the gall to, you know, take her at her word—she'll cry in disappointment. How dare you?

MAXIM EXCEPTIONS

There's a silver lining. Think of V-Day as a handy filtering process. Millions of lonely, non-boyfriended girls go to Single's Parties. It doesn't get any easier. For one, the very fact that the girl is *at* the party means she doesn't have a boyfriend, improving your odds right off the bat. And just like a wedding, this day has made her reflect on being single and lonely, creating insecurities that you can exploit. Because you're a romantic.

MAXIM #83

ALWAYS DOUBLE DOWN ON 11.

YOU ALWAYS DOUBLE down on 11. Always. When you're playing blackjack and the dealer slips you an 11, it doesn't matter if you bet five bucks or five thousand: you must double down. It's the smart move. It's the only move.

Let's consider why you wouldn't double. Pretend you have an 11 and the dealer has a queen. I'll admit. It's scary. There's a good(ish) chance the dealer gets another face card, meaning he has 20, meaning you're in trouble. And if you're betting $100 (like Jon Favreau in *Swingers*), you're tempted to play it safe, lower your risk.

Wrong. While there's a chance the dealer scores another face, there's an *equal* chance that you get a face card, meaning you'd have 21. The odds of a face are a wash, but you have the advantage (11 vs. his 10), so you should always, always press your bet. Even when it's daunting, you must do what you know is right, play the game the way it's meant to be played.

MAXIM IN ACTION

So you're wondering . . . why is this maxim in the chapter about women? What does blackjack have to do with dating?

Let's think back to the birth of this rule, to Jon Favreau and Vince Vaughn. Every guy who's seen *Swingers* (which should be *every guy*) knows that in this one particular case, doubling down was *not* successful.

To recap: Favreau (the guy who couldn't get girls) gets an 11. Vaughn (the womanizer) whispers in his ear, "Double down, Baby. You gotta double down on an eleven." Favreau's terrified: " . . . but that's two hundred dollars. This is blood money." They argue. Finally he doubles.

He gets dealt a 7, giving him an 18. (Vaughn: "Eighteen's good, eighteen's good, Baby.") Just when it looks like the dealer's about to bust, he pulls out a dagger-in-the-heart 21. Dealer wins.

The scene encapsulates the theme of *Swingers*: dating is all about making the gutsy move, even when you might fail.

He loses this hand of blackjack. And he strikes out with girls— again and again and again. (Leaving nineteen phone messages for Nicky, ruining the moment with "Dorothy," etc.) If Favreau's character had it his way, he'd prefer to quit hitting on girls, just as he'd prefer to quit on the 11. Doubling takes courage. And sometimes it doesn't pan out. But the only way to eventually *get* the girl—just like the only way to really win money at blackjack—is to fight the good fight, to make the right call—even when you might lose.

Favreau kept at it. He kept battling his fears. He kept doubling down, and he was rewarded with (then-hot) Heather Graham.

MAXIM EXCEPTIONS

It's tempting. This is tough. I'm very, very close to saying "No Exceptions." There isn't much wiggle room here. If you don't double on 11 . . . you either don't know blackjack or you don't have stones.

But there is actually one *minor* exception to this rule. And it's a sneaky, lawyerly, Jackie Chiles-esque loophole. If it's the end of the night and you've exhausted your funds, and you literally only have $5 left, and you bet it on blackjack, and you get an 11 . . . you don't have any money, so you can't double down. That—and only that—is your exception.

MAXIM #84

UNHOOK THE BRA WITHOUT HELP.

SETTLE DOWN. THIS isn't some riff on high-fiving, locker-room boasting about sex. It's not about notches in your bedpost. It's not about "scores" or getting laid. It's about the fine art of actually *doing* it, and doing it well. You need to not suck at sex.

It starts with this: you must be able to unhook a bra effortlessly. When you struggle with the bra, jerking, fumbling, yanking at the lace, either she'll lose interest or you'll lose inches.

This, therefore, is the golden key to how you can live with yourself and all your shameful, casual flings and hookups: you seek practice. You need repetition, And unless you feel comfortable asking your buddy to wear a bra, role-playing, while you caress and undress him, this means you need to date a lot of girls. As a kid, Larry Bird shot a thousand free throws every day. Be like Larry. (Iverson: "We're talking about practice. Practice!") Think of promiscuous, casual dating not as something cheap or tawdry, but rather an investment in sexual excellence, a thoughtful, heartfelt gift for the wife you haven't even met. It's sweet, really. It's romantic. It's irresponsible *not* to sleep around.

And in the worst sex analogy that you will ever hear, think of foreplay like the siege scene in *The Two Towers*. It's about buildup. The battle wouldn't work without the prefighting drama. Half the fun (for her) is the anticipation, the ratcheting up of tension, the sharpening of swords and the smiting of armor. Even in *Die Hard*, almost thirty minutes elapse before the bullets start flying.

And while we're on the subject . . . Alcohol is your ego's friend and libido's enemy. Drink accordingly. Remember the old rule of thumb: too much liquor, you finish quicker.

MAXIM IN ACTION

This isn't a joke. This is a public service announcement. Most guys really, truly have no idea how much it matters to have a basic proficiency in sex. Bad sex will kill a relationship. It will spoil an otherwise perfect third date. You know how you talk about girls *before* you sleep with them? That's what girls do *afterward*.

MAXIM EXCEPTIONS

Figure 9.4.
Courtship.

Some bras are just weird. If your girl wears something elaborate involving clasps in odd places, zippers, or silky strings tied in a clove hitch knot, you're not expected to magically know the secret. If you find yourself bumbling through one of these "virgin alarms" like Princess Vespa in *Spaceballs*, just keep your sense of humor and she'll gallop to the rescue. She's used to it. Don't take this the wrong way, but she's probably worn that corset with someone else before you, and she'll probably wear it with someone else after you.

MAXIM #85

A BUDDY'S SISTER GETS A NAME.

YOU LIKE TO refer to girls by epithets, like Indie Theater Girl or Elevator Girl or Lumpy Shoulders Girl. You'd never tell your buddy you hooked up with "Kristen"; you'd say you hooked up with Peanut Butter Girl.

So you don't think of girls by their names. It humanizes them.

A second category of girls, however, must be referred to with first names. These girls have histories and personalities and even feelings, too. They're much like you and me. They're friends of your family. Or platonic girlfriends like Cathy.

Or your buddy's sister. For these girls—the ones with names—dating is forbidden. Sex is forbidden. Even hand holding is forbidden. Your buddy's sister is *your* sister. (Except in one rare circumstance.)

Girls with names are off-limits. When you break up with girls, it always ends poorly. Always. (By definition, every relationship ends poorly—either in breakup or in death.)

Since you know it will end in a six-hour cryfest, a fight, or frosty disdain, you're unwilling to gamble your buddy's friendship.

MAXIM IN ACTION

It won't work. It can't. Let's say your friend Chucky has a smoking hot sister. For the sake of argument, let's pretend she's 24, very single, self-confident, and has once told you—with heavy eye contact and touching your forearm—that she's open to casual flings with no strings attached. One of two things can happen.

Scenario 1: it's bullshit. There's always a string. Maybe she's not even aware of it, but those pesky "emotions" will enter the equation— they always do, whether from you or her—which leads to jealous texts, passive-aggressive voice mails, and the inclusion of Chucky's sister to every guys' night-out. Which torpedoes your friendship with Chucky and splits your group into two rival camps—Chucky and all your friends in one camp, you in the other. Ugh.

Scenario 2: you *are* able to keep things casual. She's happy. You're happy. It's perfect for everyone except . . . Chucky. Think about poor Chucky. For years you've swapped locker-room stories about sexual exploits, acrobatic positions, and how you once lasted seventy minutes at the top of a jungle gym. Now Chucky will think of his sweet little sister and the jungle gym—with you, his best friend. Don't do that to Chucky.

MAXIM EXCEPTIONS

You may hook up with your buddy's sister on only one condition: you marry her. If your intentions are truly honorable, if you go beyond giving her *a* name and actually give her *your* name, too, then you've passed the threshold. It's all or nothing.

You need to ask his permission. And you need to give this some serious thought—not only do you risk your friendship, but you also risk inviting him into your family . . . forever. Pitchers of beer with Chucky is one thing. The next fifty-seven years of nuclear family is something else. Tread lightly.

MAXIM #86

FIRST DATE IS ALWAYS DRINKS.

SOMETIME IN HIGH school, you figured out that the movies make a laughably bad first date. Eye contact is impossible. You're both embarrassed by the awkward arm-around-the-shoulders thing. There's no drinking. (On the upside, there's no talking.)

You ruled out the movies, and you settled on that time-honored first date: dinner. It's time for your next leap forward: dinner's just as bad.

Follow this maxim instead: the first date should always be drinks.

Right off the bat, you save at least $80. That's the obvious perk. But look deeper. Here's the surprising, happy truth: denying the girl dinner has zero downside. None. In fact, it will actually help your chances.

MAXIM IN ACTION

If you go to dinner, one of three things can happen. Let's imagine three hypothetical dates: Stacy, Gretchen, and Candy.

Date #1: Stacy
Dinner rocks. You're charming, she's gorgeous, she laughs at your jokes. You can't believe you're sitting at the table with this blonde stunner. You leave the restaurant and it's 10:30. It's too early to go home, so you're off to a lounge to seal the deal.

Date #2: Gretchen
Ugh. She's not so cute in bright light, she won't shut up about her roommate's crippled dog, and she's already rolled her eyes at you twice. After dinner, you hug awkwardly and agree to call each other, even though as soon as you part, you both delete the numbers from your phones.

Date #3: Candy

Jackpot. Underneath the dinner table, her hand's on your knee and she's telling you about the time she kissed a girl in truth or dare. She whispers in your ear and asks if you're okay with casual sex. You skip the postdinner cocktails and head straight to the sack.

Hypothetical: What would have happened with Stacy, Gretchen, and Candy if you just skipped dinner? Let's examine each one more closely:

Stacy (She's Hot and/or Possible Action)

Good chemistry is good chemistry. Whether you're poking at salads or sipping martinis. With Stacy, dinner means $100 plus another $80 at the follow-up bar. Better to just head straight to cocktails. If you need a change of scenery, head to a second lounge.

Gretchen (She's Ugly and/or No Action)

She's already wasted your time. Why let her waste your money?

Candy (The GGW alumni)

Please. You could take her to Home Depot and you'd still be in good shape.

MAXIM EXCEPTIONS

Obviously, there's the chance that you meet a girl you actually—brace yourself—have "feelings" for, and you truly want to make the evening special, you truly want her to enjoy a spectacular dinner. (Note to every girl I've ever dated or ever will date: this exception applies to you.) Even then, though, think about drinks. Lounges offer other advantages, too. A restaurant setting can be stuffy and formal. Your date has the uncomfortable task of assessing how expensive a plate she should order—Caesar salad or the lobster? You're separated from her by a wooden table, making even holding hands seem like a treacherous, transatlantic journey. Whereas at a bar you can sink into a cozy sofa, knees pressed together. Because you're romantic.

MAXIM #87

BEING CONSIDERATE DOESN'T MAKE YOU A WIMP.

DESPITE WHAT THE other ninety-nine maxims might lead you to believe, it is, in fact, possible to be a real man without being a real asshole. Never use machismo as a cloak for laziness, pettiness, or self-ishness. At the risk of sounding like your kindergarten teacher: it's okay to be considerate—it doesn't make you a pussy. (Am I the only one whose kindergarten teacher talked like that?)

Consider relationship errands. If your girlfriend's cooking dinner and asks you to dash out and grab a bottle of wine, set the table, or even—*gasp!*—throw together a salad, it doesn't mean you're whipped. It means you're not a tool.

It's okay to be the guy who always holds the door open. It doesn't make you weak. You can be the guy who pulls out her chair, who helps with her coat, who carries her luggage. You may not, however, be the guy who carries her purse.

Ready? We're about to hit some rocky waters. It's also acceptable (encouraged, even) to ask about her day. From time to time, you might find it useful to express empathy, understanding, or mutual outrage (unless the conversation's over the phone—see MAXIM #22.)

Figure 9.7. *Carry everything but the purse.*

It doesn't make you a wimp to watch an "I owe you" Sandra Bullock or Kate Hudson flick. After you've crammed the DVR with *PTI, Sopranos*, and Game 7 from the 2006 playoffs (she doesn't understand why you selected "save until manually deleted" for a game you've already seen), it's okay to keep her company for *Project Runway*. This doesn't make you soft. It makes you a grownup.

Don't wait for her birthday to surprise her with breakfast-in-bed. Surprise her on Tuesday. Part of the reason you loathe Valentine's

Day (see MAXIM #82) is that you really *do* believe in spontaneity. This doesn't make you a pushover. It makes you a good partner.

MAXIM IN ACTION

In the sixth-most-carnage-soaked "guy movie" of all time, Mel Gibson spends his entire life clinging to a girl's flower. Is William Wallace a pussy? Then again, she gets murdered and he gets castrated. But this (probably) won't happen to you.

My father is the nicest guy you will ever meet. In a showdown he would out-courteous and out-manner Alfred the Butler. He's polite and sensitive and would roll his eyes at eighty-three of these maxims (sorry, Dad). Beneath the soft exterior, however, he has a backbone of steel and when push comes to shove . . . you will get shoved. It's one of Dad's greatest lessons to me: you don't need to be a dick to be tough.

MAXIM EXCEPTIONS

Watch out. Don't let the pendulum swing too far. Just as there's a fine line between stoicism and surliness, there's an even narrower path between kindness and clingy-ness. Short of cheating or violence, hands down, the worst thing you can do in a relationship is become smothering. You know that guy. The guy who calls her five times a day, who paints her toenails, who tucks her picture in his wallet and shows it to strangers the way John Cusack worships Beth in *Better Off Dead.* Never be Clingy Guy.

MAXIM #88

NEVER SHIT WHERE YOU EAT.

IN THIS CHARMING little cliché, your office environment—or maybe your apartment, dormitory, whatever—is "where you eat." Sex, hookups, fooling around, kissing, and having a relationship with a girl constitutes the "shitting."

You've heard it before. And it's simple enough. So let's skip to the Maxim in Action so you can learn from my mistakes.

MAXIM IN ACTION

I used to live with a stripper. I didn't know it at the time, as she answered my Craigslist roommate-wanted ad by saying she was a cocktail waitress—technically this was true—and never divulged details. In hindsight, my obliviousness was shocking: she paid her rent in cash, she never talked about work, and she loved to cook pasta in her panties.

It was only a matter of time. One night we split a bottle of Shiraz, then sat closer and closer on the sofa, and the next thing you know we were, as the saying goes, shitting.

The stripper-sex was as good as it sounds. And our "dates" consisted of her tiptoeing from her bedroom to my bedroom—sometimes in the middle of the night, sometimes on a lazy Sunday morning—cutting out the pesky dating chores like restaurants, picnics, and movies. A dream realized.

That lasted two weeks. Then something began to change. Instead of the impromptu hookups, she'd ask, "What are we doing tonight?" And she would call me at work. We talked about our days. We kissed each other goodbye in the morning. We cuddled. And then one day it hit me . . . I don't have a sexy roommate who I get to hook up with—I have a wife.

The damage was done. You can't unring that bell. Even after we had "the talk" about how we probably made a mistake—how we should revert back to just being roommates—those prickly "emotions" were injected into the apartment. The vibe became frosty. I dreaded coming home from work, afraid of the thick, heavy air of resentment. (It really was like marriage.) The only honorable solution was for me to leave—I couldn't kick *her* out; that didn't feel right—so I found a new place. The last weekend of our cohabitation, I finally connected the dots and realized she was a stripper, which led to her showing me some "work outfits" and telling stories of how she hooked up with her fellow stripper girlfriends . . . which led, of course, to a relapse.

The final score? I had two weeks of free stripper sex. In exchange I lost my apartment, my home, and yes—my kitchen—the literal place where I eat.

MAXIM EXCEPTIONS

On the other hand . . . here's the thing about shitting where you eat. We literally do it all the time. Think about it: our culture now has modern plumbing. Your kitchen is probably less than twenty feet from your bathroom. The pipes are all connected. Contemporary workforces are now prepared for contemporary relationships, so while intra-office romances are frowned upon, they're usually not forbidden—unless there's untoward behavior. Just be prepared to flush the toilet.

MAXIM #89

EVEN THE TRAIN HAS DIGITS.

MEAT MARKETS, CLUBS, and bars are only so much sport. It can get tedious. The crowd is sloppy drunk, the girls are grinding into each other, and their tops are flimsier and tinier than a handkerchief.

Sounds miserable, right? Okay, so no one's complaining. Nothing wrong with shooting dogs in a barrel. The modern man, however, should know how to exploit his natural surroundings—outside the sexually charged bubble of a traditional "scene"—to strike up conversations with girls anywhere, anytime, whether in the elevator or in the bagel shop.

As an example, consider the train. When you play it right, the Amtrak is a moving buffet of women. Unlike an airplane, where you're stuck in 24B and wedged between a fat dude and a rotting grandmother, you can choose where to sit. Scan the passengers. Sit next to the cutest girl. She's yours for the next two hours, providing what amounts to a free, impromptu, no-pressure first date.

Timing is key. If you board the train too early, most rows of seats will be empty, so it'll look awkward (and creepy) for you to plop down right next to her. Rookie mistake. Instead, wait until half of the passengers have boarded—at least one person in every row—so you have a legit reason to join her. Sit down, smile, say hi. Make eye contact. You have a built-in shared perspective: no one likes to travel. Exploit that. Use it to build rapport.

Or think about the Laundromat. There's nothing less sexy than liquid detergent and fabric softener. Use this to your advantage: girls are relaxed, without their usual defenses, and available to talk for a thirty-minute wash-and-rinse cycle.

Or the museum. At venues like museums and galleries, you accomplish two things: (1) you preselect a pool of girls with greater merit; (2) you have plenty of easy conversation starters. You're both staring at

Figure 9.9.
Single's scene.

197

the same painting, for God's sake. If nothing else, you can nod at the painting and ask, "What do you think?" Aaaaand you're in.

MAXIM IN ACTION

Another venue worth exploring: sporting events. Careful. As per MAXIM #13, the primary mission of watching the game is to *watch the game.* Don't get too cute. That being said, if you can flirt with the girl while fulfilling your sacred duties as a fan, you've immediately found someone with a common interest, you can dazzle her with your knowledge of the cover-2, and your shared rooting will give you both the temporary illusion that you might be right for each other.

MAXIM EXCEPTIONS

Obviously if you're happily in a relationship (for now), you are exempt from this rule. The key, however, is that you do have the *ability* to meet girls outside the typical meat market. You never know when you'll need it.

MAXIM #90

YOU DON'T CHEAT.

THERE ARE MANY reasons to ditch a girl. Maybe she has odd elbows, maybe she chews with her mouth open, or maybe she has too much hair on her forearms. All good reasons. If you're unsatisfied with Forearm Girl—whether it's been two weeks or two years—then end it, but end it honorably. Break up. Cheating isn't manly, it's weaselly. You don't cheat. Period.

But let's say you cheated. You blew it. Let's say it was a drunken "accident." (It wasn't. It's still your fault. Don't blame this on tequila.) In this example we're not talking about some enduring, premeditated affair, we're talking about a sloppy night of passion.

Guilt floods your body. You can't sleep. You debate the pros and cons of telling the truth. You sweat. You can't think straight. Shit. You want a time machine. You want to undo this. You regret this more than you regret anything in your entire life. Dammit. What do you do?

You talk to your buddies. Here's what they say.

MAXIM IN ACTION

Imagine that you have two best friends, Matt and Graham. Matt's the nice guy. Graham's the scoundrel.

MATT: You need to tell her the truth.
GRAHAM: Fuck that.
MATT: You have to. Every good relationship is built on trust.
GRAHAM: That's selfish.
MATT: How is the *truth* selfish?
GRAHAM: Because if you tell Forearm Girl—
MATT: Can we please call her by her name? Her name is—

GRAHAM: Oh Matthew. Never call 'em by their names. I told you it only humanizes them. Forearm Girl will—

MATT: Call her Sarah.

YOU: Can we get back on subject?

GRAHAM: Right. If you tell *Forearm Girl* the truth, it's selfish. You're just dumping the guilt onto her, unburdening your conscience and inflicting her with pain.

MATT: But she's his girlfriend. Doesn't she have the *right* to know? If you buy a used car, you have the right to know that the engine doesn't work.

YOU: Hey. My "engine" works just fine.

GRAHAM: You bet it does buddy. Look. You fucked up. And your punishment is to live with this secret, bury it, for the rest of your life.

MATT: This is wrong.

GRAHAM: It is. But the wrong has already been done. You've already made one mistake. Don't make two.

YOU: I want to do the right thing.

Awkward pause.

GRAHAM: Listen, buddy. You had the chance to do the right thing . . . and you didn't. What's done is done. That ship has left the building—

MATT: How can a ship leave a building?

GRAHAM: Work with me, Matt. Look. You've already driven the bus to Wrong World. We're there. But if you tell her the truth, it will give you a false sense of morality—

MATT: It's not a *false* sense, it's the right thing—

GRAHAM: But if you drop the T-Bomb—

YOU: T-Bomb?

GRAHAM: Truth Bomb. The T-Bomb kills everything. You. Her. The relationship. The T-Bomb is nuclear.

MATT: So he needs a . . . radioactive suit?

YOU: I'm lost.

GRAHAM: Look, do you care for this girl?

YOU: I do.

GRAHAM: Do you want to hurt her?

YOU: I don't.
GRAHAM: You've armed the bomb. Don't drop it.

MAXIM EXCEPTIONS

As for the core rule "You Don't Cheat," it's the only maxim that has a one-word exception: "None." No exceptions. There are, however, many different tactics—all of them flawed—on how to handle the aftermath. It's never tidy. The scenario between Matt and Graham, obviously, is about an unmarried, relatively uncomplicated dude. But when houses, wives, and kids are involved, you're in a different ballgame. And you probably need a different book.

PART X.

AND DON'T FORGET . . .

YOU CAN NAME AT LEAST FIVE SUPREME COURT JUSTICES.

A MAN SHOULD be well informed. How can a man govern himself if he doesn't know what governs him? Not just "government" in a textbook, three-branch-system use of the word, but also the forces of power—economic, cultural, political, artistic—that mold your world, impact your job, and etch the contours of your generation. Plus you'll impress chicks.

Another perk: An interest in current events helps you age gracefully. As we get older, our gusto for clubs, womanizing, and 4 A.M. bacon-eggs-and-cheeses will naturally wane, and we'll hunger for something else to pass the time. Sports help. Books help. Family helps. Porn really helps. Current events, though, are the nouns and verbs of a grown man's vocabulary.

MAXIM IN ACTION

A laughably incomplete list of news-ish stuff that every man should know:

The basics of the Middle East conflict. I know, I know, you didn't crack open this book for a history lesson. Don't worry. This'll be quick. There's actually a third certainty besides death and taxes: what happens in the Middle East will impact you (whether you know it or not) for the rest of your life. Even if it's not flared up, it's always there, just lurking beneath the surface, it will never go away. Like herpes.

The (rough) status of the Dow. A basic understanding of what's affecting the Dow requires, by definition, a grasp of market fundamentals. You should know what's happening with the economy, and not just whether it's "up" or "down." Careful though: don't be Portfolio Braggart Guy.

The actual platform of your party. Left, right, red, blue, libertarian, anarchist, socialist, monarchist, Colbertist, whatever—you need to know your shit. Vote for whomever you want. Ideally, though, you have a sense of what your party believes, why they believe it, and where you disagree. It'd be nice if you knew more about your candidate than that you'd "like to have a beer with him." I'm a fun guy to have a beer with. I wouldn't be the best president. (Then again I might not be the worst . . .)

Figure 10.1. *You know things.*

The Supreme Court justices. If you can name the entire fifty-three-man roster of the Tampa Bay Buccaneers, you probably have the capacity to remember the names of nine old grouches. It's not that their "names" are important, per se, and this isn't just a cheap parlor trick. It's a litmus test. If you're following the moral and legal clashes of our time— gay rights, torture, whether we should abolish the DH—these are names you know.

MAXIM EXCEPTIONS

Youth. I used to be apathetic—cartoonishly ignorant, even— about current affairs, and I wore my vapidity as a badge of honor. In 2004, when a friend barged into my apartment to tell me, breathless, that "Howard Dean dropped out of the campaign! Holy SHIT!" my response was, "Who's Howard Dean? And what'd he drop out of?" I got my news from only one source—SportsCenter—and I figured that if any news was *sooo* important that it would personally affect me, then I'd see it when they interrupted ESPN. (Ironically, this theory was darkly vindicated in the fall of 2001.) So what happened? The same thing that happens to every guy: I grew up.

MAXIM #92

NO SHORTS AT A FUNERAL.

AS COVERED ELSEWHERE in the maxims, you care less about style than substance. So it's tempting to think that when you go to a funeral, the important thing is that you grieve for Aunt Edna; what counts is the depth of your grief, not the length of your slacks. Who cares if you're wearing a suit or a Hawaiian shirt? Either way she's dead. And given all the other shit he has to worry about, probably, God isn't sweating whether you're in wingtips or flip-flops. Besides, didn't Jesus wear sandals?

But this isn't about the Big J. It's not even about Aunt Edna. This is about respect. Despite all your other selfish, socially unacceptable quirks (see the other ninety-nine maxims), at certain moments in life, you have the ability to submerge your ego, respect tradition, and swallow your pride for something greater than yourself.

Other quasi-annoying traditions that you must follow:

Gifts at Weddings

Guilty. For a while I assumed that because my buddies were my buddies, we didn't *really* care about the pesky tradition of wedding gifts. It's just a friggin' set of cutlery, right? But I forgot one key variable: the bride. It doesn't matter if you just bailed him out of jail; if you flub the wedding gift, this drives a wedge between your buddy and his wife, and therefore between your buddy and you. Keep it simple, respect the registry. This is one gloomy case where formality trumps friendship.

Visiting Your Grandparents

It might not be your textbook definition of "fun." It might require skipping games, missing parties, even blowing off women or sex. So be it. As you get older, a core plank of manhood is supporting and entertaining your grandparents. Besides, the older they get, the more embarrassing dirt they dish on your parents.

Beer for Your Buddies

Even if you're not planning on drinking, when your buddy hosts a party or just invites you over for the game, you must bring a six-pack. This is the male version of flowers. There are precious few formalities between grown men, and this one's inviolable.

MAXIM IN ACTION

One more bit of etiquette. As per MAXIM #9, you have a healthy skepticism for birthday gifts. But when someone pops a baby, your role is to shower that child with every manner of toy and bauble. The kids are easy to please. They'll cherish any hunk of plastic that costs ninety-nine cents at the gas station. Just remember, when you see your buddy's or your sister's toddlers, you may never show up empty-handed.

MAXIM EXCEPTIONS

Maybe the deceased wasn't a suit-wearing kinda guy. If your surfer buddy Chaz—a pot-dealer and "performance poet"—died from a toxic overdose, perhaps the best way to show your respect is a midnight bonfire where everyone wears kilts. Your mission isn't to slavishly follow the cookie-cutter rules of decorum; your mission is to respect the departed . . . even if means a box of Twinkies at three in the morning.

MAXIM #93

HATE THE FONDLER,
NOT THE PHONE.

THERE'S NOTHING WRONG with loving gadgets (see MAXIM #65 on technology). You have—or you crave—the latest iPhone, Black-Berry, Sidekick, or some gizmo that synchs to your car and lets you steer it remotely.

Play with it. Geek out with it. Load it with software that sounds indispensable, like the iPhone's "unit translator" that lets you convert—wherever you are, anytime!—fluid ounces into cubic centimeters. Thank God for this new application. What did we do before it?

The etiquette of "phone talking" you already know. But there's a new rule: you may not turn into a "phone fondler."

A phone fondler is a guy who has his BlackBerry glued to his palm. He's always stroking it, reading it, typing on it, caressing it. If it's out of his sight more than thirty seconds, he panics, freaks out, like Gollum and his precious.

To avoid being The Fondler, you must follow these three rules:

(1.) You may not look at your phone more than you look at the other people in the room. It appears sulky and even bitchy. You become less interesting. If your head is always bowed down, creepily illuminated by the soft electronic glow, you're as useless and invisible as Ronnie on *The Shield*. Who's Ronnie? Exactly.

(2.) You must minimize your test drives. If you just got a shiny new iPhone that's the envy of your friends, it gets real old real fast when you give a detailed walk-through of every new feature. We get it. You have a fancy phone. There's a fine line between sharing your enthusiasm and flaunting your wealth.

(3.) You may not keep a Bluetooth in your ear. Using a Bluetooth headset is fine. Using one in public (the grocery store, say) is frowned upon but permitted. Using one *when you're not on the phone*—keeping the fucker dangling on your ear—is item #26 on the global rankings of douchebaggery.

MAXIM IN ACTION

One more rule that many guys violate: you may not use your phone as a table decoration. Don't keep it out in front of you, prominently displayed, as if it's some magical artifact that commands the group's attention. If you're expecting a critical call, just flick it to vibrate and keep it in your pocket. The phone-on-table is like putting a stack of hundred-dollar bills on your plate and gazing at them fondly.

MAXIM EXCEPTIONS

If you've been lassoed to a social, family, religious, or work function that's in clear conflict with a more important sporting event, you may check the score with impunity. Let's say someone has the audacity to schedule a rehearsal dinner on Game 7 of the World Series. You are in the right; they are in the wrong. Discretion is optional. Follow the game.

MAXIM #94

YOUR DOG MUST BE LARGER THAN A TOASTER.

DOGS ARE THE only outlet for men to show affection. You can pet them. You can play with them. You can have long, sprawling conversations with them, pleased at their lack of response.

There's only one rule with dogs (actually there are more; see below): it must be larger than a toaster. Not clear enough? Five signs that your dog is too small:

(1.) You are unable to play Frisbee with your dog, because when he tries to catch it, the Frisbee bowls the dog over and smacks him to the ground.

(2.) On an airplane, your dog comfortably fits underneath the seat in front of you.

(3.) Try as he can, his cutesy, itty-bitty legs can't quite make it up to the couch, so you've installed a Barbie-doll-size step for him.

(4.) He cowers from squirrels.

(5.) At least once a day you almost step on him because he's too tiny to register on your peripheral vision.

Not too long ago, dogs were primarily used for hunting, for chasing down your prey—triumphantly returning with a carcass in their teeth. You don't have to actually be a hunter. And you don't have to actually own a hunting dog. But you must remain faithful to the spirit of man's best friend: he's a vigorous companion, not a toy.

While we're on the subject, some other iron-clad rules:

- No matching sweaters.
- No dressing your dog up for Halloween.
- Never even *think* of sending him to a doggie yoga class.

- No Santa suits.
- No outsourcing—you and only you may train your dog.
- No "gourmet" snacks that require more than ten seconds of preparation.
- Even if she's a girl, your dog should not be clad in pink.
- No collars from Prada or Marc Jacobs.
- When you leave your dog at a kennel for the weekend, it may not involve a doggie massage or "kiwi bath."

MAXIM IN ACTION

On the one hand, they're becoming more mainstream: we see these Chihuahuas and teacup-sized puppies everywhere we look. They've arrived. On the other . . . the place we see them is in *Us Weekly*, *TMZ*, and "Page Six": in the arms of Britney Spears and Paris Hilton.

MAXIM EXCEPTIONS

If your name is Arnold Schwarzenegger and you're the guy in *True Lies*, you are allowed to have a tiny little puppy. This is because you also ride a motorcycle through a shopping mall, leap onto a flying helicopter, and slaughter thirty terrorists.

If your name isn't Arnold Schwarzenegger, you still have a loophole. Let's say your girlfriend already had one of these toy dogs before you moved in, making you a co-owner. You're off the hook. In this situation, however, your appropriate response is to also get a 230-pound Saint Bernard that will relentlessly intimidate Tinkerbell.

Figure 10.4.
The food chain.

MAXIM #95

KEEP HER OFF THE POLE.

HIS POLITICAL RANTS? Take them or leave them. However, you must concede that Chris Rock introduced the most fundamental, most elemental rule of parenting: your mission as a father is to keep your daughter off the stripper's pole.

There are many safe, loving, nurturing parenting techniques to raise your daughter properly. These aren't them. Instead, these are the four drastic, draconian measures you're willing to take to guarantee that she will never change her name to Destiny. Courtesy of my buddy Cody, one of the world's best 2 billion dads:

(1.) **Harp constantly on how smart she is.** I don't care if your daughter is too dumb to finger-paint. I don't care if she fucks up play dough. Does her syntax and diction remind you of a cat being slowly strangled by that dude in the Scream painting? Talk about how hard it is to make up a new language and praise her creativity and forward thinking. A woman's likelihood of dry-humping a pole is inversely proportional to how smart she *thinks* she is. You will raise a genius, even if she's the first genius with an IQ of 76.

(2.) **Tell her she's fat.** Seriously. Tell her that she's really packing on the pounds, no matter how skinny she is. Get her afraid to show her body to anyone, anytime, ever. Will this scar her? Will this damage her? Will this make her hate you? Yes, yes, and yes. Then again, anorexia/bulimia vs. gonorrhea/chlamydia is not a hard call.

(3.) **Raise her in an insanely devout religion.** You could be an atheist. You could be a Buddhist. That's irrelevant. If you pour your daughter a stiff shot of Jesus—the fire and brimstone kind—what you lose in Sunday mornings you get in peace of mind.

(4.) **Send her to boarding school.** True[1] stat: 96 percent of sex workers have some kind of "Daddy issue." How can your precious angel develop a daddy issue if Daddy's in another state? As an added bonus, if it's an all-girl school the chances of her being a lesbian increase. While this hurts your chances for grandchildren, this increases your chances of not killing her boyfriend when you catch them humping in your car.

MAXIM IN ACTION

Successful practitioners of these parenting techniques include Mr. Hilton, Mr. Spears, Mr. Simpson, and Mr. Lohan.

MAXIM EXCEPTIONS

Obviously, these are not the ideal tenets of your parenting. If possible you'd like to raise her without lying about her intelligence, without deporting her, without intentionally chunking up her belly, and without turning her into Tammy Faye. If you can employ conventional techniques that keep her away from the champagne room, do it. The point is, you're willing to get your hands dirty, you're willing to look like a bad guy, and you're willing to have her hate you. Someday she'll thank you. Or maybe she won't. But at least she won't be thanking Gus for buying that second song.

---

1. This stat might not be true. But it seems plausible, right?

MAXIM #96

YOU CAN (MOSTLY) USE A SET OF BASIC TOOLS.

THE IMPORTANCE OF tools is fairly well worn territory—high five, Tim Allen—drills, chainsaws, rah, rah real men yada yada. So we'll leave it at that.

Instead, here's a little secret: thanks to the fruits of specialization, you're no longer required to reroof your own home, mount Sheetrock, or install a new water heater. Let's not bullshit ourselves, okay? That's why we have construction workers.

But. And it's an important but. While you get some wiggle room on the old-school "real-man" tool-time nonsense, there remain some basic, around-the-house tasks that you must be able to competently execute:

Unfuck the toilet: The less we dwell on this visual the better, but in this unfortunately real-life scenario, you must be self-sufficient. You can unclog, you can turn off the water, you can fix the handle, you know how to handle the gasket.

Chop down a tree: How often do you actually get a chance to shout to the world, "Mother Nature Is My Bitch!" Chopping down a tree is joyful. It's the reassertion of the triumph of man, the power of your spirit, the rightness of your cause.

Figure 10.6.
Conquer nature.

Properly hang a heavy painting: And not just the flimsy ones that need a wimpy nail. But a real piece of art—a heavy son of a bitch—that needs to get mounted. You must know how to hook picture wire on the back of the frame, properly distribute the weight, and navigate the drywall.

Mount a Christmas tree: Not the plastic pieces of junk. The real ones, the shedding and dripping and pain-in-the-ass ones, the kind that Ralphie's dad wrestles with in *A Christmas Story*. You can saw off the trunk, trim the branches, install the stand, and keep it (more or less) vertical.

Paint: You don't need to be Banksy, but you should be able to competently paint a living room or bedroom. (Obviously, the only acceptable color is white. See MAXIM #2 on colors.)

Fix the fuse: This falls into the category of technology (see MAXIM #65).

MAXIM IN ACTION

If you rent an apartment, your skills will atrophy and you'll soon lose self-reliance. One day you're fixing fuses and installing new porcelain sinks, and just a few months later you call the super to change a light bulb. So remain vigilant. When possible, do it yourself.

MAXIM EXCEPTIONS

If water damage has corroded your linoleum tile floor and you need the sucker replaced, there's no shame in calling the Linoleum-Tile-Floor-Replacer-Man. Seriously. It's okay. Why should you squander your hard-earned weekend on an ugly, thankless, endlessly frustrating task? It's time we stand up to the outdated notion that "real man" means "real carpenter." There's nothing wrong with carpentry. It's an honorable profession. My grandparents built their own houses from scratch, practically with bare hands and a stack of lumber. My dad spent two years single-handedly gutting his basement and turning it into a professional wood-working shop. And I love him for it. But that was their generation; this is ours.

MAXIM #97

IT'S ONLY A FLESH WOUND.

PAIN? WHAT PAIN? You don't feel it. Just like the knight from Monty Python, you're not really hurt; it's only a flesh wound. It doesn't matter that your arms are chopped off and your legs are bloody little stumps. You can still bite.

The root reason? If we cop to pain, then we concede our own fallibility, which means that there's an outside chance that sometime, somewhere, we did something wrong. This is unacceptable.

And on top of this . . . men are secretly rankled by the conventional wisdom that *women* are tougher because women, and only women, can go into labor and give birth. This is the ultimate trump card. We haven't figured out how to beat it. So every day, in ways big and small, men do everything we can to refute the irrefutable.

We're equally unfazed by emotional pain. Childhood scars? Ridiculous. It's better to bury that pain inside, bottle it up, and then unleash our fury when it's least expected and most unwarranted.

Truth time. We do feel pain. Lots of it. Just not where you'd expect. Moments when men feel pain:

Getting beat by a girl. It's true. Our ego is so fragile, such a delicate flower, that when we lose to a girl at tennis we'll silently weep. We've failed as a man. We suck. We're humiliated. We don't deserve our penis.

Getting ditched by a buddy. Maybe he's kidnapped by a wife. Or maybe he moves away. We'll never admit this to anyone—certainly not to our best friend—but this cuts deep. We're wounded. We miss him. When we see him again, however, we'll just nod our head and say, "They should bench the QB."

Getting bad reviews. A girl could call you a coward. She could say you're selfish, dumb as a doughnut, a prick, and the worst thing that's ever happened to her. She wants you dead. She could say all that . . . and it wouldn't bother you much. That wouldn't have nearly the devastating, ego-melting impact of her saying, "The sex was only mediocre."

MAXIM IN ACTION

"And here comes . . . Willis Reed!" It still sends chills. Or Emmitt Smith against the Giants in 1993 with a season on the line, rushing for 168 yards with a separated shoulder. Michael Jordan and the flu game. And so on.

As boys, we grow up watching these heroes flout medical advice, instilling the lesson that we, too, should risk our health by playing through pain. We want to be like Mike. So we try. Too bad we don't have his health insurance.

MAXIM EXCEPTIONS

Obviously there's a time and place for admitting pain. Simple enough. But even *then* sometimes the true heroes—the ones who really matter—will inspire. Every guy knows these role models. For me, it's two grandfathers who first fought Hitler, then fought cancer. In one particularly rocky stretch of treatment, a nurse asked Grandpa to describe, on a scale from 1 to 10, the intensity of pain. The man was in agony. Eighty years old—recipient of multiple Purple Hearts—and now he couldn't breathe, laugh, speak, or twitch a muscle without lightning bolts of pain. He looked at the nurse and calmly said, "Four."

MAXIM #98

CARRY YOUR BRIEFCASE.

A BRIEFCASE IS a time-honored staple of manhood. It's iconic. For millions of cube dwellers, it's the modern-day lunch bucket, a tool belt, a symbol of doing a square day's work for a square day's pay.

It doesn't matter what you put in your briefcase. It can be filled with actual work documents, gym clothes, a turkey sandwich, comic books, or a year's supply of condoms. It can be brown, black, leather or steel, pricey or cheap. That's up to you.

There is only one rule: you may never wheel your briefcase. I don't care if it's heavy. I don't care if you're on an eighteen-hour journey from Des Moines to Zurich. You have no more reason to wheel your briefcase than you do to ride the senior shuttle at the airport. Butch it up.

More sympathetic voices might wonder, "Wait. But how is wheeling a briefcase different from wheeling a suitcase? Is *that* forbidden, too?" Fair question. While it's preferable that you carry your luggage without the use of wheels, the ubiquitous

Figure 10.8.
Future roadkill.

airport "roller bags" have changed the game, erased the taboo. So why's a briefcase different?

Because this—the briefcase—is our final stand. A line we must not cross. As our culture has grown cushier, softer, and more dependent on technology, we've lost all connection to our primal physicality. We no longer gallop on horses, we cruise-control in Hondas. We no longer tend our crops, we tend our databases. We don't hunt bucks, we play Buck Hunter.

After centuries of global tranquilization, holding your briefcase with a firm grip, a steady shoulder, is the very least you can do. It's our gender's last flag of dignity. Don't burn that flag.

MAXIM IN ACTION

If you're on the street and you see a wheeled briefcase, chances are it's being held by a kindly old grandmother. Or maybe a small child. Women often wheel laptop bags, and there's nothing wrong with that.

When you see a grown man wheeling a briefcase, chances are he's using his other hand to play with his BlackBerry, he's cutting in line, and he's sucking up to his boss on a Bluetooth headset. Do you want to be that guy?

MAXIM EXCEPTIONS

Airline pilots wheel around those blocky rectangular file boxes. It's part of their uniform, so it's permitted. What if it's some sort of bulky, specialized work bag full of gear, like DJ equipment or electrical apparatuses? Acceptable. The theory here is that this bundle is so heavy, so awkward, that you should really be using a *car* to haul the bitch around, and you're actually taking the manlier route of lugging it on foot. And no, your laptop does not count as a "work bag full of gear."

MAXIM #99

FIND A CLOSER SPOT.

YOU HAVE A human radar that detects open parking spots. You're never wrong. So you never settle; you keep searching for that perfect space. This infallible, almost supernatural ability—maybe it *is* supernatural, who can say—allows you to cruise past rows of wide-open, perfectly reasonable spaces that your wife or girlfriend will shriek at, pointing, whacking you upside the head, wondering why you've been circling around for twenty minutes when we've passed a gazillion spots and the concert is about to start and if we'd taken that one, back there, or maybe that one, or that one, or hell even that one, we'd already be in our goddamn seats.

Your other uncanny driving abilities:

You always have the right of way. Some drivers are just *bonkers*. They don't even see you when you speed through the red light, and their recklessness could get someone killed.

You're not really speeding. Yes, you were pushing thirty miles over the speed limit, but that doesn't mean you were *speeding*. The car is in control. Besides, what causes accidents is the "speed differential" between the two cars, not the speed itself. (This is actually true.) And if the officer gives you a ticket, it's simply "bullshit" regardless of the circumstances. Fifty-seven miles per hour in a school zone? They don't get it. There are kids in that school zone—*kids*! Your mission, therefore, is to get out of that school zone just as fast as possible so you're safely out of harm's way. If your hand is in a fire, do you sloow-wwwly remove it?

You're a legendary multitasker. You can scarf down a chicken burrito without dripping guacamole, send a text message, find a better song on the radio, and program a new address into the GPS (not that you need it, see MAXIM #7) without taking your eyes off the oncoming car in front of you.

MAXIM IN ACTION

One summer I was in four car accidents. Luckily only two were my fault; in the other two I was asleep, so you could hardly blame me. You can't fault the driver when he's not even awake, right? I mean, what could he possibly do to prevent the situation? Let's be reasonable. I finally decided to move to New York and abandon driving forever. I'd had enough. There are too many bad drivers out there.

MAXIM EXCEPTIONS

Sometimes there are no other cars in the parking lot. There's an ocean of empty spaces, which fails to present a challenge. Now, in this one instance, will you take the first available spot. This spot happens to be farthest and least convenient. As Clark Griswold would say, "You'll be the first to leave."

MAXIM #100

NEVER BLINDLY FOLLOW
RULES OR MAXIMS.

THE PHRASE "RULES are made to be broken" is cute and all, but under the slightest bit of scrutiny, you can see that it's sort of horseshit. That's like saying "ice cream is made to be melted." Just because ice cream *can* melt doesn't mean it should. Rules are made to be followed. Without rules we have anarchy, bloodshed, and the 2005 Minnesota Vikings.

A less catchy but more accurate slogan: "Rules are meant to be followed . . . but what counts is the spirit of the rule, the context of the rule, and awareness that from time to time, disparate rules will come into conflict, in which case, you should follow the more global, more transcendent rule." Now where can I get that bumper sticker?

You might have noticed a few—I'm embarrassed to use this word—"themes" in these maxims. What's important is adherence to those themes, not whether you pack two pairs, three pairs, or seven pairs of shoes in your luggage. The real stuff (like cheating) matters. The small stuff is there as a guideline, not ironclad edict. That being said, there's really no excuse for packing seven pairs of shoes.

Okay. Awkward time. I'm about to drop some emotional, gooey, soft, and feathery words that neither of us likes to say in public. The themes include junk like integrity (faithfulness to your woman, succeeding at work through merit), fidelity to your friends and family (backing them up in a fight, treasuring your kids), valuing substance over style (no fake tans, no highlights), self-confidence (you can wear pink, you can be sensitive, you're open-minded, you're not homophobic), self-improvement (you throw a tight spiral, you know how to flirt, you read Melville), and, most important, not being That Guy.

MAXIM IN ACTION

The ultimate confession. At one point or another, I've probably shattered at least ninety-five of these maxims. I've left early to beat traffic. Sometimes I've been so swamped with work, so out of touch, that I didn't even know who was pitching. I tried yoga. (In my defense, I didn't get it, didn't like it, never tried it again.) I used to have toe fungus. My sense of direction is so awful, I once got lost driving home from high school; I love GPS, it's the best. I get cold. I once counted calories.

So how do I sleep at night? Are the rules null and void? Absolutely not. I believe in the overarching principles, I believe in the underlying message, and I believe that despite a single lapse in judgment—or ninety-five lapses in judgment—we all have a shot at redemption.

MAXIM EXCEPTIONS

This one. This maxim is the only exception to the maxim: "Never blindly follow rules or maxims." (Chew on that little paradox.) Everything else is negotiable. My buddy Evan once gave me a piece of advice. I had a thorny ethical dilemma involving love, friendships, betrayal—it was a heavy, gut-wrenching decision—and I badly needed his help. I explained the whole mess. He took it all in, silent, reflective, wise. He sat in stillness. The wheels turned. Finally he looked me in the eye and said with devastating candor, "Jeff. I think you should use your judgment." I nodded, letting that sink in. He's right. He nailed it. That's what it's all about. Judgment. I shook his hand and thanked him. We parted.

Hours later it occurred to me that this was the most useless advice I've ever received. Use my *judgment*? *That* was the sage advice? That's worthless! It's just a wise-sounding way of saying, "Huh, I dunno know; good luck with that shit, kid."

So these are my parting words. When you are uncertain over which maxim to follow, when you are in doubt, when you need clarity, you must use your judgment.